From Drowning in Debt to Financial Freedom

How to Bail Yourself Out of a Financial Mess by Building a Home Party or Network Marketing Business

Susie Nelson

Here's what others have to say about Susie Nelson's training and coaching:

My business has become so much more productive and "alive". Before these trainings, I was doing things with my business and my team to the best of my ability. Once the training started, I realized that I was not utilizing my time, talent and efforts in the most effective ways possible to continue the momentum I needed to move into the highest leadership levels with my company. I now find that my stress level is much lower due to the tools I have been provided to make my business work for me instead of me working for my business.

Dondrea Bryant - Sr. Director, ThirtyOne Gifts

I started my direct sales business about four months before I found Susie's training courses online. To try to obtain growth for my business, I had signed up to do a number of vendor events and, having no sales experience whatsoever, searched online for some guidance. I ordered Susie's 'Kick Butt Booths' training course and was so pleased with it that I contacted her directly with additional questions. From the moment I spoke with Susie, I knew she would make an amazing business coach and mentor. I immediately made the investment and signed up for her professional coaching program. It's only been a couple of months and my business has more than doubled in size. Using Susie's advice, I saw instant results! I now have a team of consultants and more bookings on my calendar than ever. While my company has tons of training, I found it to be too overwhelming and, frankly, not as useful as the guidance I've received from Susie. Susie has taught me how to book shows, how to have conversations about my business, and how to train new consultants. She breaks everything down and makes it so simple, anyone can achieve success by following her formula! If you are in the direct sales business and are looking to grow your business, Susie's coaching program is for you! Sign up...you'll not be disappointed!

Tara Murray, Independent Star Stylist, Stella & Dot

Taking a class with Susie Nelson is life and business changing. Fantastic presentations, personal attention, and everything you need to take your business to the next level. Susie has a way of taking the business and breaking it into easily duplicatable steps, and you can learn at your own pace. Highly recommend!!

Beth Millman, Independent petPro, pawTree

I was feeling overwhelmed with all the pieces of running my network marketing business. Taking Susie's training has helped me get organized and learn how to simplify the steps to my business. I now feel confident to train others on my team how to keep it simple using the skills of inviting, booking, follow-up and training! Such practical skills, thanks Susie!

Heather Gall, Young Living Essential Oils

Susie Nelson has been one of the best mentor/ teachers I have ever had. Her 8 week course has had a huge impact on my mindset about my Direct sales business. I now see myself sharing an opportunity with women not bugging them. Tremendous value! Susie's experience and honest opinions has you feeling a true connection immediately. I love sharing in the community with other direct marketing consultants and the feeling of support is vital in this business. I will always recommend Susie Nelson, she's the real deal. My sincerest gratitude for sharing your wisdom.

Kristine Dutra, Independent Stylist, Ruby Ribbon

I met Susie 2 years ago. A novice to the industry, she is exactly what I needed. Kind yet tells you what you NEED to hear. Firm yet always encouraging. Her information is clear, smart, doable, logical. In short, if YOU DESIDE to push through your own fears and do exactly what she tells you to do, you WILL succeed!! Excited, frustrated, impatient, happy, hopeful, not sure, positive. Do these emotions feel familiar? Susie helps you work through all of them!! Susie is and will always be the coach who believes in you more than you believe in yourself. She is smart so you be smart. Invest in yourself and hire Susie. It is the best decision I ever made! Thank you Susie I am honored to be mentored by you and be your friend.

Mary Ann Metcalf, Independent Director, Melaleuca

Taking a leap of faith and jumping heart-first into one of Susie Nelson's trainings and one-on-one coaching has been the best thing I have done for myself and my business so far! Susie is a mecca of experience in the Direct Selling World and she takes her experience and helps make it applicable to my specific business and my expertise. Her feedback and challenges to me have really made me take a close, hard look at myself and my business and I will be soaring! Thanks Susie!!

Sharon Prince, VIP Spa Consultant, BeautiControl

I have been really blessed to have known Susie Nelson for nearly 20 years now. We worked together in a former business where she became my mentor and dear friend. Last year, I reconnected with her to utilize her business coaching services to help me with my new business. From our very first consultation, she skillfully guided me to really focus on what I could work on each week to make my business thrive. I was making myself stress out over all the things I wasn't doing with this business; but her uncanny ability to attentively listen to my specific situation and then suggest some very simple potential possibilities totally turned me around! I honestly believe breaking my overwhelming list of 'things to do' down into manageable daily or weekly tasks was most helpful. Taking her advice, I advanced my business within the first month of coaching. Most of us have some pretty amazing skills; but when you add the remarkable talents of a coach like Susie to keep you focused—you just can't help but soar to new heights! I would recommend Susie to anyone I know who is looking to gain that extra competitive edge to succeed in whatever business they are in—she is simply exceptional!

Linda Robinson, Independent Director, Melaleuca

From Drowning in Debt to Financial Freedom
How to Bail Yourself Out of a Financial Mess by Building a Home
Party or Network Marketing Business
© 2014 Susie Nelson

CONTENTS

Foreward

Sharing this "how to advice," based on what I learned from the financial mess that I created, then overcame, has actually been a painful experience. It felt like I was re-living all of my mistakes over, and over, and over again. But if it can help - even one person - to change their "financial life" as a result, then it's all been worth it.

Years ago, I attended a special session at a business conference with a brilliant business coach — Tracy Quinton. During the class, she asked each participant to develop their "personal mission statement."

After much anguish, a few tears, and some prompting from Tracy, I realized what is most important in my life. My personal statement is:

"Who I am is Freedom"

For me that means freedom of all types, but most importantly – ***Financial Freedom.***

It took me several years to manifest my personal mission, and, as you'll read in the following pages, I dug myself a huge financial hole as my ultimate form of self-torture.

I think it's pretty safe to say that you purchased this book, looking for a way to dig yourself out of a big financial pile of crap, as I did. You'll only accomplish that goal by starting and continuing to take action. And, as with any behavior that you have to change, it is a process whereby you may take a few steps forward, and a few steps back along the way.

I certainly have...

I've learned some tough lessons. From the bad programming and bad habits I had to change, and most of all the interesting — what I now call "relationship" I had with money.

I'm going to share the process I went through to take control of my finances. If you think about it - it's really pretty simple. If you bring in more than you spend each month - you've got money leftover. You can use that "surplus" to pay off debts, save for retirement, and put it to work to build your personal wealth.

One way to make this process happen faster is by joining and building a home party or network marketing business. Unlike a part-time job, where you'll have set hours and an hourly pay; being in direct sales gives you the power to be in control - of your time, your schedule, and your income.

It is not a "get rich quick" industry. Building a successful business will take dedication, a willingness to learn, and some work. But it can be your route to financial freedom...**IF**...

And that is a "big IF"...

...**IF** you manage your business finances and business decisions well.

If you take your same poor money management habits right along with you to your home party or network marketing business - you will simply dig yourself a bigger hole.

But if you manage your business well - from Day One - and use your profits to impact your financial future - that's gold.

For full disclosure, I am an expert in the industry. I'm a coach, trainer, and author.

It might sound a bit "self-serving" that I encourage people to start a home party business, since you could be one of my potential clients. And in some respects, that's true.

I quit my full-time engineering job to build my business, built that business to annual commissions in the six figure range ($105,000 to $135,000 to be exact), but also made a lot of financial mistakes through that process. Painful financial mistakes.

That's why I'm passionate about teaching you how to build your business the right way. Learn from my mistakes, change the way you manage your finances, and put whatever profits you earn - whether it's $500 per month, $5000 per month, or much more - to work, benefitting your life for the long-term!

So let's get started.

It won't be easy, but I want to urge you to go the distance. No matter how bad it seems today, pull yourself up by your bootstraps and dig in. I'm living proof that it is possible to make dramatic changes – and what I know – once you take control of your finances, life will never be the same!

Financial Freedom can be yours, too!

Introduction

Death is inevitable – a fact that we all know – but don't always like to contemplate or acknowledge. Although fate will determine how we meet our final destiny, I think we all secretly hope that, after a long, bountiful life, we drift away to the heavens while asleep in our beds.

A couple years ago I realized that, at a very young age, I was dying a slow and painful death. I was drowning. I wasn't in the ocean or in a pool. Nor was there an intruder in my home, ruthlessly holding me under water in the bathtub as I thrashed for my freedom. Instead, I was drowning without being in water at all. I was being sucked under the raging current by financial debt.

Each day I'd wake-up feeling exhausted after a sleepless night of worrying about my bills and lack of resources to pay them. The stress was so overwhelming that getting myself up and out of bed became an unbearable struggle. Mind you, normally I would jump out of bed at 5 a.m., eager for the experiences of a new day. But not anymore.

I no sooner got started with my day when my "financial tsunami" would hit me with full force. It included phone calls from creditors and collection agencies, a mailbox full of collection notices, and big scary looking men knocking at my door to serve me with the latest legal notification.

If you're dealing with a big financial mess yourself, you'll understand this stress. There is no reprieve and no escape. The anxiety keeps getting stronger and it tries to overtake you; and the harder you try to tread water and gasp for your next financial breath, the more overwhelmed you feel.

There's no end in sight, there's no life preserver within reach, and the lifeguard is permanently off-duty.

Exhausted both physically and mentally, you reach a point where you want to succumb to it – let the tide whisk you away and put you out of your misery.

But financial drowning doesn't work that way.

Instead, you worry about your lack of money every single moment of every single day, and you feel the life being sucked out of you slowly – painfully – helplessly.

When the sun rises in the morning, it doesn't signal a fresh start. It's just a signal that you can start gasping for another breath.

You don't know where to turn for help, and the harder you fight the rushing current of bills and creditors, the worse it seems to get. It's a lonely battle, too, because you're too embarrassed to talk about it with family and friends. Besides – when people know you're struggling financially they suddenly treat you as though you're afflicted with a rare and highly contagious disease.

I understand the reaction. Considering my past behavior, I'm sure my friends were leery about my motives and intentions. My behavior left them on a very unsteady high-wire – should they feel sorry for me, help me (i.e. enable me), or simply avoid me? I messed up a lot of relationships due to my poor relationship with money, and most can never be repaired.

So I want to be your "BFF" through this process. Stay focused - even when the going gets tough. I believe in you - I'm living proof that you can take control of and change your financial life forever. You've got this.

Why I Wrote This Book

I'm not a financial planner or an accountant. For that matter, I have no connection to the financial industry. Instead, I'm a person who has made nearly every financial mistake possible in my life.

I made the decision to write this book because I figured out how to take control and change my finances. I figured out how to stop drowning in debt and start living. I want to be the financial lifeguard who, not only drags you out of the pool, but teaches you to swim.

I know what it feels like to be bombarded with phone calls from collection agencies; I've dealt with the stress of having my home foreclosed; and I was totally embarrassed when my car was towed away by a repossession company while I was at work. I was the queen of bounced checks (I wish I had just 10% of both the returned check and overdraft fees that I paid to my bank).

In addition, I was self-employed, and for several years I did not pay estimated taxes, or, for that matter, manage my business finances well. As a result, I built up a gigantic Federal tax debt (to the tune of nearly $200,000). If you think dealing with collection agencies is "fun," try dealing with the IRS. But more about that later.

Sharing all of this information with you is still quite painful. I only do so to help you understand when I tell you that I've made lots of financial mistakes, I'm not kidding. I'm not some "expert," who wants to tell everyone what to do, but has never really experienced the pain themselves.

There's one additional "financial war story" I need to share. Back in 2002, I filed a personal bankruptcy. There's many things I wish I could undo, but if a magic genie would grant me one wish, I would ask to erase the bankruptcy from my past – not because of the negative impact on my credit report, but for a much more personal reason. Filing bankruptcy robbed my soul. The self-loathing that, for me, was the direct result, was worse than anything I have ever endured.

For lack of a better description, I can only compare it to the "death eaters" in J.K. Rowling's Harry Potter books.

You know -- those scary creatures that overtook a person and literally sucked the life out of them.

That's what it felt like to go through the bankruptcy process. Couple that with the fact the attorney I hired was a complete moron (another lesson – you get what you pay for), it was a devastating experience and I recommend that you avoid it, if at all possible.

As you can see, I didn't just struggle to deal with my bills – I did it up big. I created a financial pile of crap. Sounds blunt? Absolutely. And I only share it so you understand that I definitely have walked in your shoes.

My hope is that you aren't dealing with the enormity of financial problems that I did (I created them and I'm fully responsible for them. Let me make sure I'm clear about that.) But if you are – read on.

As I battled with my financial challenges, I often went looking for advice. I have a whole shelf full of books from all of the financial experts – Suze Orman, Dave Ramsey, Jean Chatzky, David Bach, Robert Kiyosaki, Ric Edelman and many more. In their books and during their personal appearances, they make some excellent points, and I learned some great ideas from all of them.

But when I was so overwhelmed that it was easier to ignore the bills and the calls and live in a world of denial.   I didn't feel most of the financial gurus truly understood the hopeless feeling of not knowing where to start; or that desperate, helpless gnawing in your stomach when the voice in your head tells you that you'll never become financially solvent; or being so overwhelmed by the pile of bills staring you in the face that you become lethargic. You know you're alive, but you also know that this isn't "living."

I had to figure out how to take control of my finances, because, quite literally, not doing so was killing me.

It isn't easy. There is no pixie dust or magic wand that will make it all better in an instant. The gurus made it sound like I could take a few simple steps and - poof – my finances would be fixed.

That approach never worked for me – and I'm guessing it won't work for you.

I often joke about my lack of great cooking skills. My ideal recipe would include details like "open the top of the box" so it would be almost impossible to fail.

That's the kind of detail that I share with you in this book.   When your head is whirling and you feel overwhelmed, follow the instructions so staying on track is a "no-brainer."

If you're like me, you invested in this book as one last shot – one desperate, final attempt to find the advice that will work – and, perhaps, hoping to find someone who really understands what it's like to be harassed every minute of the day by creditors and collectors; who knows that it sucks to get turned down for credit cards and car loans; and who knows what it feels like when a banker pulls your credit and looks at you as though you are lower on the food chain than pond scum.

I couldn't find the help or the answers in the dozens and dozens of books that I read, so I had to find my own solutions. If
investing in this book is your final cry for help to change your financial picture once and for all – then grab onto the rope – these techniques were my life raft in my financial storm. They worked for me, and I believe if you're ready to take action and implement them, these ideas will work for you.

Are you ready to change your financial life?

When you say that you're ready - I have to ask — are you **really really** ready? If you've reached the point where you are so fed up with barely scraping by that you can make a solid, no holds barred commitment to go the distance; if you're prepared to follow these steps to take charge of your finances once and for all; then get ready to start implementing new techniques <u>today</u>. Not tomorrow; not next week. Start now.

If that's not you, then grab another pint of ice cream, tune into another rerun of some reality TV show, and never pick up this book again.

Sounds harsh, I know. But you won't make lasting change that impacts the rest of your life unless you are ready to engage.

I learned from a guy named Bill Glazer that "The difference between people who succeed and people who don't succeed is *implementation.*"

Bill is right — *especially* when it comes to changing the bad habits and poor behaviors that got you into this financial mess.

Make a commitment to start now — and get off the couch - it's time to take action.

Here's What We're Going to Do:

I want this book to help you change your life - quickly.

So here's what we're going to do:

1) You can't make dramatic changes unless you really take a hard look at how you got into this financial mess in the first place. I share my story, and recommend you take a close look at yours, too.

2) Next, I'm going to take you through, step-by-step:

a) how to organize your bills

b) then, how to prioritize which bills get paid first, second, and so on…

c) How much you make, versus how much you spend. (It's a real eye opener.)

d) My list of ideas for cutting expenses - just to get your creative juices flowing.

3) Meet Helene Leonard. She shares her story of how she and her husband, Joe, dug themselves out of a huge financial mess. Truly inspirational.

4) Living within your means is important. But why not get yourself out of debt, and on the wealth building track FASTER by starting a home party or network marketing business?

I'm going to share the reasons why I feel this can be a great option for you.

Plus - you'll see information about several different businesses that I recommend you check-out.

5)   Now that you're adding a new business, it's important to manage your BUSINESS finances well, too. I'll give you my simple tips.

How Did You Get into this Mess?

I sat, numbly, on the couch, watching yet another rerun of "Law and Order," but honestly could not tell you one detail about the program. All I could think about was what a loser I was (thoughts, by the way, that aren't going to help you change your finances). I think I was in shock. How did a woman who has two degrees and a well-above-average I.Q. end up in this mess?

Poor financial management has cost me dearly in my life. I have ruined relationships, lost friends and family, and lost lovers over money issues. And when I'm stressed, I eat. Plain and simple. I packed on an additional 100 pounds having ice cream and pizza "pity parties" over my finances, and every single pound represented financial stress and worry.

The first step for me was to take an honest look at the past and to take responsibility. I must warn you that if you choose to do this exercise (and I highly recommend that you do – it's one of the first steps), it isn't easy and it isn't fun. But it's important.

As I started to look at my past and at my financial programming, I kept picturing Dr. Phil sitting in my living room telling me it's time to "get real" about my finances and my lifestyle. Frankly I wanted to give the guy a good swift kick in the groin (true confessions – in my dreams, or should I say, nightmares, I DID give him a big boot in the gonads). But here's what I learned through my honest self-evaluation.

Yes – get out the violin – my lack of financial management started when I was young and, although I'd love to blame my parents for my poor choices, trying to shift responsibility to them for the mess that I created would be cowardly. I decided that I strictly need to understand the dynamics to facilitate change. (Did I mention that I'm not a financial planner or accountant, and let me add that I'm NOT a shrink!)

OK, so the childhood "stuff" – my Dad worked two jobs all of my life – full-time school teacher by day; full-time insurance adjuster by night.

My Mom worked out of the house – typing for the insurance adjusting company. Considering how much they earned, my parents still lived from paycheck-to-paycheck because our family had all of the toys – the lake home in Wisconsin (and all that goes with it such as boats, a snowmobile, and a big budget for entertaining), several horses (that we boarded at the local stable), and a private airplane — to name a few.

I was taught the fine art of worrying about money at a very early age, since the "centerpiece" on our kitchen table was a big honkin' calculator. My Dad woke up early each morning and started going through the checkbook, figuring how many hours he needed to bill at the insurance adjusting gig to cover the next month's worth of expenses. And, since he was a social character, he often dragged my butt out of bed to "talk" – which really meant he wanted me to refill his coffee cup on-demand and punch the numbers on the calculator.

Dad also had a problem with alcohol that he never addressed. Was he a full-fledged alcoholic? Who knows – he passed away in 1995 so at this point – does it really matter?

For the purpose of me understanding my bad relationship with money – yes, it matters. Unfortunately, when my Dad drank, he wasn't a very nice guy. (For the record, when he was sober – he was a funny, generous, great guy. But not true when he was drunk.)

Through it all, I learned a very destructive pattern. It

went like this: Dad gets drunk, Dad acts like an ass and screams, yells, pounds on the table, and tells me I suck. Next day, when sober and feeling guilty, Dad spends money on me to "show me that he loves me."

My parents also worked very hard and worked all the time (a pattern I now recognize in myself). I'm thankful that I learned their work ethic, but at the same time, when you manage money well, there should also be a healthy balance of work time and free time to enjoy yourself.

Let me re-emphasize – I'm sharing this story with you, strictly because I had to get an understanding about the conditioning behind my poor financial behaviors. I believe that kind of comprehension is necessary to move forward. I don't sit around all day blaming my parents for all of the problems in my life; the list of good things they provided for me would far outweigh the list of not-so-good. But this "get beat up emotionally and then get rewarded financially" pattern that was established for me at a very early age continued into my adult life. Recognizing and changing this pattern was just as important (if not more so) as opening the mail and balancing my checkbook.

As I grew older and no longer had my Dad to give me a lip lashing followed by his "I'll show her that I love her with money" rewards – I got even "smarter" (she says facetiously) and started to figure out how to beat myself up instead. And, to be frank, I have screwed up every relationship in my life by creating a financial mess, so I could turn to the people in my life to bail me out, to "show me that they cared about me."

Understanding the pattern is a start – but changing the behavior and replacing it with new habits takes even more work.

And to make matters worse, I chose to pursue my own business, and several years ago quit my job (with no planning, no transition, no savings, and a boatload of credit card debts) to build my business on a full-time basis.

I had help from lots of people – my boyfriend, Dennis (a guy I should have married, but I'm sure my poor money management was a big reason he never asked).

I created the perfect conditions to really manipulate the people who cared about me with the excuse that I needed financial help while I was building my business. But when they loaned me the funds, I made extremely poor choices about where I spent them. I was operating my business like a bad episode of "Lifestyles of the Rich and Famous" and the money was gone as quickly as it was loaned to me.

My "so-called" business expenses included spending big bucks on airfares, hotels and rental cars to travel around the country, renting expensive meeting rooms, and buying expensive "incentive gifts" for business associates in my organization. All of these activities were poor decisions and not smart business.

The business I chose to affiliate myself with was a network marketing company that sold women's clothing through home parties. Despite my mismanagement of my business finances, and making the business a thousand times more difficult than it needed to be, I managed to build one of the top organizations in the country and the majority of my income was based on receiving residual commission checks monthly.

The fluctuation in income, due to the cyclicality of the business, proved to be an added financial challenge. Each month, I looked forward to the 15th – the day that my commissions were direct-deposited into my checking account. And by the 17th – the money was usually gone (I told you, I'm a master at beating myself up!). That would start my "scrape-by-for-a-month" cycle all over again.

Unfortunately (and yes, fortunately!), after growing to $140 Million in annual sales at its peak, that company made several mistakes and started to die a slow and painful death. (All of the lessons learned from that experience could be the topic of another book.)

In June, 2008, they ceased operations – a day I fondly refer to as the "day my income died." Since I'm single, it was the day that I learned I would not receive commissions a week later (money that was already spent), and, as an independent contractor, the day I realized I would not qualify for unemployment benefits. Perhaps it was my personal "black Monday."

When that company closed its doors, it accelerated my trip down a road that I had already traveled on for many years. It caused me to hit my financial "rock bottom" on that fateful day – I either had to make some rapid changes, or throw in the towel and start looking for a big cardboard box under a bridge.

That was the day I made the decision to change my financial life, and I started taking action immediately.

So what's your story? What has impacted your poor financial choices and gotten you into a mess?

Take time to think it through - not to beat yourself up - but to get clear of the poor choices and bad behaviors that you need to change - now.

You might even start a "Financial Freedom" journal to record your thoughts.

Financial Freedom versus Barely Scraping By

Let me tell you what financial control and financial freedom feels like.

On the most basic level, you no longer spend any time or energy worrying about money. Your days of tossing and turning all night, stressed over how you're going to make your mortgage payment or scrape up a couple bucks for your kids' school lunches, are gone.

Taking control of your finances has an even greater impact on your life that goes far beyond getting a good night's sleep or having a few bucks around the house.

If you are like me (or like I used to be), you probably check the available balance on your credit cards daily, or at least before you use the card (I often called to check my available balances from the car in the parking lot of the store.)

Now you'll be able to shop with confidence, and you'll pay for your purchases with your debit card so the cash is immediately withdrawn from your checking account. That feels really great!

Worried about how you'll help your kids get through college? Now you have a plan in place, and you'll be confident you can finance it.

Need to buy a new car? When you are in control of your finances, you will walk into the dealership from a position of power. You'll be able to negotiate a great deal, and if you are *choosing* (note I said *choosing*) to finance the vehicle, you will qualify for the very best interest rates. If the dealer doesn't cooperate, you'll walk away, knowing you will do business with an auto dealership that will give you a better (fair, but better) deal.

Want to take your kids on a vacation? When you manage your finances well, you have the funds for your family vacation before you go on the trip, and you spend your vacation enjoying the experience, rather than worrying about the bills that will be in your mailbox before you arrive back at home.

Another one of the many benefits of financial freedom is your ability to take advantage of investment opportunities. Let me give you an example. In recent years, there have been some incredible opportunities for real estate investors, due to the high inventory of foreclosures on the market. When you are in a position of financial strength, these are the types of investments you can evaluate (using help from qualified professionals) and possibly invest in, if the numbers work.

And probably the biggest benefit of financial freedom – no more fear of the future. Now you are saving and planning for your future. It won't be left in the hands of the politicians who haven't figured out how to save the Social Security and Medicare systems from bankruptcy yet. Instead, you'll confidently know that you can take care of yourself.

You'll also really enjoy watching your savings, investments, and net worth grow. When you've taken control of your financial life, you'll feel powerful, self-confident and abundant.

How Badly Do You Want to Change Your Financial Life??

I'm going to teach you some simple steps that you can take immediately, if you want to change your life badly enough.

I feel I need to harp on this. If you are strictly giving lip service to the people in your life, then forget it. You will not succeed. But if you are willing to dig in and take action, then you can get on the path to financial freedom right now.

So here's your next assignment:

Grab a piece of paper and make a list of the 25 reasons why you **need** to change the way you manage your finances and get out of debt (notice I said **need** rather than **want**).

I know, 25 will seem like a stretch, but what you'll learn from this exercise is the reasons you come up with towards the end will

probably have the most punch. The first dozen are easy (I'm sick of worrying about money, I want to pay off my debt, I want to be able to shop, I want to buy a new car – whatever) – but when you dig deep and figure out exactly why you need to make this happen, it adds "umph" to your motivation to keep taking action.

What is it that really keeps you up at night? What makes your stomach churn?

As I started to really get clear on my reasons for changing, things such as "to have better relationships" and "to eliminate fear from my life" came up on my list.

Spend time, right now, preparing your list. I know, you might think it's a hokey project, but clarity is important here. You may even want to discuss your list with your spouse or significant other. Don't stop until you have at least 25 reasons listed.

Once you have this list completed, you're ready to continue on to the next step in this process.

Let's Get Started – Take Action NOW!

I'm going to warn you – the steps are simple, but this won't be easy. Most things in life worth doing aren't. Think about it, giving birth isn't easy, either, but women do it everyday. When the going gets tough – pull out your list of 25 reasons why you *NEED* to change you finances (that you just created) and review it often to renew your passion.

I will teach you the techniques to make the process manageable. There will be days (like this one) where you'll want to scream, you'll want to throw in the towel, you'll want to go out and spend money you can't afford to spend (or, do as I did -- eat a pint of Haagen Daz and order a pizza).

Bad financial behavior won't change your life. Taking control and managing your finances WILL change your life.

As you take control of your finances and put yourself in the driver's seat, you will start to feel empowered – and that feels good. You'll feel strong; you'll feel on top of the world. And you'll know that you can confidently deal with most any financial obstacle that gets thrown at you.

Let me be candid. This next statement might get under your skin – that's OK. I won't be helping you if I'm not honest with you. So here goes:

It's time for you to grow up – financially, anyway.

Yes, whether you choose to be mature in other aspects of your life is irrelevant. Starting now, you will become a "financial adult." You are in charge of your financial destiny. You can choose whether you continue to drown in bills or you learn to swim – even if it's up stream. It's time to take control, and as I said, grow up.

I've broken the process down into step-by-step pieces, so you'll have no excuse to delay. Start now.

Here are the Steps to Change your Financial Life:

Step One: Get a clear understanding of what drives your bad financial behavior.

What are your bad money behaviors and where did they come from?

Right now you're in "survival mode" so we can't spend a lot of time on this, but it is important to understand.

Write down your answers to these questions:

1) What were your parents' attitudes about money, and what did you learn from them about money management?

Did they say things like "Money doesn't grow on trees," or "money is the root of all evil?"

2) What are your bad money habits? (Do you bounce checks, not balance your checkbook, not open the mail, etc.?)

3) When you're bored, depressed, or not feeling good about yourself or your life, do you go on a shopping spree?

4) Do you regularly buy lottery tickets or go to a casino?

5) Do you and your spouse or significant other disagree about your finances?

6) Do you ever over-spend to get back at your spouse?

7) When you're stressed about money, what do you do?

8) When you were younger, did you learn any bad patterns (as I did) from your parents?

The goal here is to get an understanding of the bad money behaviors that you have – not to place blame. Write down any additional observations you have about your relationship with money.

Step Two: Accept Responsibility for your Financial Mess.

This is critically important. No matter what kind of conditioning you experienced, you have to take responsibility for your mess. Yes, you were probably taught poor money management behavior by others who influenced you years ago, but now you get to choose whether or not you want to continue to let others have that hold over you.

Let me ask you this question:

Do you want to continue on as a victim, letting others have control over you and your life, or do you want to be powerful by acknowledging that you created your financial mess? You can take control and you can become financially free! Which would you prefer?

Earlier I asked if you are really, really ready to take control of your finances, and since you've continued to read on, I'm assuming your answer was a strong "yes." I know you can be successful. You may not be ready to believe that about yourself, but I believe it about you.

I know – you might be saying, "It's my spouse's fault – not mine." That kind of cop-out is just not acceptable. You were part of the "system" that allowed that to happen, so that means you still have some responsibility (and not accepting that will only delay your financial freedom).

OK – enough of the "psychobabble" – as I stated earlier – I'm not a shrink – if you, or you and your spouse, need professional help to deal with these issues – by all means, get help.

Step Three: Flip Your Mental Switch

I need to ask you to trust me. This step is going to take some conscious effort – but it is a critical step that can dramatically speed up this process.

Starting right now, I want you to create a list of the money that is flowing to you – I call it the "money attraction" list.

Set-up a 3-ring binder or notebook where you can keep a daily record.

From this day forward, every penny that you receive gets recorded in the book. I'm not just talking about the money you receive in your weekly paycheck. I mean all of it – a friend treats for lunch – that's money that flowed to you indirectly. You find $5 bucks in the pocket of your jeans – write it down. You see a penny on the street – pick it up and add it to your log.

I liken this activity to "flipping a mental switch," just like you can flip on a light switch.

When you've been living in the world of financial lack, all you think about is lack. And, based on the scads of research about how our subconscious mind works, what you think about – especially with the frequency and, more importantly, the negative emotions you have when you're broke – you'll produce just that – more of the same – lack. You'll continue to be flat broke with no "pot to piss in" and your financial sink-hole will keep getting bigger and deeper, because that's what you think about all the time.

Like I said, you may think I'm nuts. Remember, I asked you to trust me. This has nothing to do with your religious beliefs (although some would argue that praying is quite similar). Considering my indecisiveness about religion in my own life, I would never be so presumptuous to discuss it with you. For me, this is strictly about quantum physics and energy.

I promise, I'll explain more later – but right now we just need to stay on task. Start your "money attraction log" now! Don't delay! Do it now. And something I also recommend that you do: each time money flows to you, and you're writing it down in your log – acknowledge it and be grateful for it by writing "thank you" next to each entry. Gratitude works wonders!

I know, your immediate reaction will be to say in your head (or to your spouse) "this chick's nuts – I'm broke – what do I have to be thankful for" – but I need to ask you to trust me here. To change your financial life, you have to start to focus on the money that is flowing towards you, and it will be even more powerful to be grateful for every penny.

Keep your "money attraction log" close-by, too, and review it often. The more you see that you do have money flowing to you and through you to benefit others, and the more you appreciate it, the more that money will flow to you. (Remember – I asked you to trust me.)

There are a few basic concepts that you also need to understand about money.

First, it's just paper and energy. They print the stuff in big, secure buildings in six locations throughout the country (Denver, Philadelphia, Washington D.C., West Point, Fort Knox, and San Francisco, to be exact).

Money is intended to flow – to you, through you and on to

benefit others. Holding onto EVERY penny tightly is not the best way to attract more. (No – I did not just tell you to go shopping! More details about this later.)

There actually is a lot of it around. Perhaps right now you're not doing a great job of attracting it, but as you take action, that will change.

For now, start your "money attraction log" to acknowledge it and become more aware of it.

Step Four: Stop going further into debt – NOW.

I'm sure you just read that statement and immediately the little gremlins in your head said "I can't do that." You're charging your daily living expenses – such as gas and groceries – and you can't survive without continuing to charge…or so you think.

Fact: You will never start to dig yourself out of this mess if you don't change your behavior.

Stop creating additional debt NOW!

Just for today (sorry to sound like a recovery program, but in many respects, this is recovery), don't go further into debt. Don't use credit cards, don't write checks unless you have funds to cover them, and don't borrow from a friend or relative.

If that means that you can't go out for dinner with friends, or have to tell the kids "no" to the movie, or have to make dinner at home rather than swinging through the golden arches, then so be it. These are the kinds of choices you have to start making right now to change your life.

Your mission: Just for today, do not do anything that puts you further in debt.

We'll worry about what will happen tomorrow -- tomorrow.

Step Five: Start saving immediately.

I know – you're broke. You don't have an extra dollar to your name, so how in the world are you going to start saving money immediately?

This step in the process is also critically important because it is how you start to shift yourself to a position of power and control over money, rather than letting money control you.

Even if you can start by saving $5 per week (although I will be encouraging you to work towards saving 10% of your income, for reasons I'll explain later), this will be a good start.

Let me tell you about my friend, Allan. He worked hard all his life in a job that didn't pay a lot of money, and had a couple part-time jobs to make extra cash. He always lived well under his means. In his day job as a barber, Allan earns tips. Once a week, he collects his tips and takes them over to the bank to save the money.

It would be easy money to blow because it isn't a huge sum, but since it is money he can't necessarily count on, and because he really likes his money, Allan chooses to save it.

(And by the way, I think he is now a millionaire – or close to it!)

Whether you open a savings account where you put in $5 per week, or stash the cash in an envelope in a drawer – I don't care (at least not at this point in the plan) – but start saving immediately.

And even more importantly, you have to make a commitment that you will not tap into the funds, except for **extreme emergencies**. Needing $20 for pizza on a Saturday night is <u>not</u> an emergency. Not having cash for gas is <u>not</u> an emergency - it's a temporary inconvenience. If someone needs urgent medical attention, that's an emergency, but not much else.

I even recommend that you start a savings log. Look at it often, and be proud of yourself – even if you start by depositing five bucks per week.

Step Six: Create and Implement your Action Plan for Financial Success

I nearly called this section "get organized" – but that is a phrase that makes me break out in hives. If I have to wait to start anything until I'm "organized" – trust me, it will never happen. You don't have to be an organized person to manage your finances well – you just have to develop a few good habits.

Right now – I want you to dig up the following:

- A couple pens or pencils
- Index cards (or squares of paper – anything will do)
- A paper bag (for recycling materials)
- A calculator. If you don't have one, borrow one. A $5 calculator will be a good investment (provided you don't keep it on the kitchen table!) but for today, get your hands on one – even if it is bright pink and has children's characters on it.
- Some sort of storage box and files (and if you don't have either of them handy, for now grab a shoebox and some rubber bands).
- Table space (or floor space – any spot where you can sort things into piles)
- The beverage of your choice (for me, that would be a tall glass of Merlot or a big cup of coffee)
- All of the stacks of unopened mail that you have floating around the house. Look carefully. You will probably find unopened mail in piles in your bedroom,

in a home office, in your car, in the garage, on the kitchen countertop, perhaps buried under magazines, in the bathroom, or crammed into the mailbox. (Did it surprise you that I know this – remember, I have "been there, done it.") You MUST – right NOW – dig up every piece of unopened mail and pull it all together – for now, in a pile.

- If you are computer savvy – grab your laptop – especially if you use Excel. If you don't – that's NOT a problem. You don't have to know how to turn a computer on to take control of your finances.

I know the unopened mail routine well, but let me share a better story about my friend, Candice (who unfortunately passed away a few years ago from breast cancer).

She was a sweet, smart, unique character and spending time with Candice was always an adventure. Like me, she was in complete denial about money management.

Candice invited me to her home one afternoon for a glass of wine, and she offered to pick me up. Her car (like mine) was loaded with junk – so much so that I had to sit in the back seat. When we pulled into her garage (which was also loaded with junk) I saw several plastic grocery bags piled on a workbench in her garage. They were bags full of **<u>unopened mail.</u>**

Later, her neighbors stopped-by carrying a bottle of wine and some appetizers. They talked about the remodeling project underway at their home, and as they pointed things out through the window, I noticed a row of electrical outlets on the outside wall of their house.

Out of curiosity, I asked Candice's neighbors if they put up a lot of Christmas lights, or what they did with all those plug-ins. Their response, "Candice doesn't pay her electric bill until they shut her off
– and that usually happens on a Friday afternoon, so her power is out for the weekend. Rather than running extension chords through our window so she can keep her refrigerator, television, and other electric appliances working, we added more outlets so she can just plug herself in."

Like I said – people in our lives do interesting things to enable us. Certainly your neighbors aren't letting you plug yourself in, right?

So back to the task at hand; have you pulled together the list of items I described?

If your unopened mail stacks are as big as mine were, this next step may take up to four hours. Don't let that become an excuse. START NOW and keep going until you are finished! Right now. Turn off the television, tell everybody to stay out of your way, because this is your time to take control of your finances.

You are going to **open and sort** your mail. Sounds simple enough - here's how you do it.

First, on the index cards or small sheets of paper, write out the following categories of the various type of bills you receive by mail:

- Household bills (mortgage or rent, electric and gas, water, garbage, insurance, homeowners association, property tax statements, etc.)
- Other household utilities (phone, cell phone, cable television, internet)
- Medical and dental (doctor bills, dental bills, prescriptions, health insurance premiums)
- Car Payments
- Other Car Expenses (insurance, gas, maintenance)
- IRS, back-taxes, student loans
- School Tuition

- Credit Cards

- Collection accounts

Next, start opening the envelopes. Put each bill on the appropriate pile, and put the empty envelope into the recycling bag. Obviously the "junk mail" can go into the recycling bag, too.

I suggest that you do this fairly quickly. Think of it as a game. How fast can you get all of these bills opened and sorted? All you are doing at this step is opening up your mail and sorting it into piles. It doesn't matter what is written on each bill – after all, it's just paper. What *does* matter at this stage is that you have taken an important step by opening the envelopes.

Until you complete this step, do not read any further.

Or, as they say in one of my favorite games, Monopoly, "Do not pass go – do no collect $200" until all of the mail is opened and sorted into piles.

At this stage in the process, you will have a tendency to start beating yourself up. I know this from experience. So I need to take a short "time-out" to explain the concept of "gold stamps." I learned this from a mentor of mine – a guy by the name of George Raynault.

Each time you do something well – in our "mail opening and sorting" task, (in this case, opening each envelope, and putting it into the appropriate pile) mentally give yourself a "gold stamp."

I equate it to a chart we had in my Kindergarten glass. We had a list of skills on a chart, such as tying our shoes, counting to ten, reciting the alphabet. When we demonstrated the skill successfully to the teacher, we were rewarded with a sticker on the chart. (And financially right now – you are in kindergarten – but don't despair – you'll be moving up a few grades very soon.)

Start – immediately – giving yourself imaginary gold stamps for even the tiniest action steps you take financially (like opening the mail and sorting it into piles!). See your pile of gold stamps getting bigger and bigger and pay attention to how good it feels when you give yourself that "gold stamp" pat on the back.

Then, in the rare instances that you mess something up – you get to cash in your imaginary gold stamps – *guilt free.* That's right – *guilt free.*

This is another technique to help you shift your mental focus from beating yourself up to recognizing yourself for the things you do well. I believe this is powerful because we all tend to fixate on what we screw up. We put our energy into beating ourselves up for an error, rather than paying attention to the thousands of things we do well every single day.

I am confident that giving yourself imaginary "gold stamps"
throughout every action step you implement during this process can help you take and maintain control of your finances much faster. It will keep you focused on what matters at this point – moving ahead and creating new habits – rather than what you messed up in the past.

Now that you have all the mail opened and sorted (congratulations!) I need you to make a commitment – perhaps a contract with yourself – right now, and that is:

"I will never let the mail go unopened again."

Yes – from this day forward, make a commitment to open up every bill and every piece of mail regularly.

Here's what I recommend to deal with your mail. Collect it from your mailbox every day, and sort out the bills from other mail. Next, find a special location in your house where you put the bills each day. If you have a desk where you can use one drawer for this purpose then dedicate that drawer as the place where you put the bills. If you don't have a drawer available, a shoebox will work.

Once a week, preferably at the same time each week (to make it a habit), you will open each bill (like you did today), update your Financial Freedom Worksheet (more about that in a minute), and deal with the bills you are paying this week. This should only take 15-20 minutes, half hour at most, when you are dealing with it weekly.

Some additional important points about handling your bills:

1) Don't put them in a location where you spend a lot of time or where you'll see them a lot. Remember, we don't want you thinking about lack. You are managing your finances, opening the mail, and dealing with your bills regularly each week. You are now taking control and managing your finances. Well done!

2) Don't keep your bills in your bedroom, especially in a location where you'll see them before you go to bed. I want you to have "sweet dreams," not "financial nightmares."

Instead, tuck them in a shoebox and put them in the corner of a closet if you have to. You'll be looking at them weekly, and that will be sufficient.

Now – for the part that is a little tougher. (Suck it up – you can do this.) The next step in the process is to actually look at the bills and create a list, using my Financial Freedom Worksheet.

I have a sign in my office that reads:

"Thou Shall Not Whine"

Do you wish you didn't have all these bills? Yes. Would you like to wiggle your nose and make them all go away? Yes. Do you feel angry, stupid, embarrassed, and down-right irritated about these bills? Yes. Or, possibly, are you mad at others in your life (like your spouse) for helping to create this mess? Maybe.

I'm not a financial planner, an accountant, or a therapist. If there are family issues that contributed to this mess – then get help. Plain and simple.

For the task today (which is taking inventory of your financial situation), letting yourself get caught up in all of those emotions isn't going to help the process.

As an ex-boyfriend of mine used to say, "It is what it is." (That
phrase, and a great recipe for gin-and-tonics were the only
two valuable things that came from that relationship – but
that's a whole different book!)

Stay on task, because this next activity will change
your financial life.

I've created a special "Financial Freedom Worksheet"
(it's an Excel spreadsheet) to help you track your finances.
You can download it by going to:

Blastawayyourdebt.com

if you don't have Excel or access to some type of electronic
spreadsheet, then get some paper and make ten columns.
First, we'll be working with eight of them. Label the columns
from left to right as follows:

Column One: Priority

Column Two: Bill / Creditor

Column Three: Amount of Monthly Payment

Column Four: Remaining Available Funds (after
paying the bill - more about this later)

Column Five: Past Due Amounts

Column Six: Due Date

Column Seven: Total Balance Due

Column Eight: Interest Rate or APR

All of this information will be extremely beneficial as we create your strategy to get out of this mess.

First, I want you to fill out the very first line with a priority of "1" – and that is savings. As I explained earlier – even if that is $5 per week – that's $20 per month. Don't over-commit – that would be setting yourself up to fail; if it's $5 bucks, then it's $5 bucks. Fill that amount in first. (The Financial Freedom Worksheet will figure out monthly savings, based on what you fill in for weekly savings.)

Now, go through the bills, one stack at a time, and fill out the information in each column, from every bill that you just opened, in the following order (If you already have these bills set-up on automatic payments – something we will discuss later – pull this information off your most recent bank statement. Also, keep in mind that this is strictly looking at the bills you get in the mail. We'll be adding other payments after you complete this task. If you don't have the information to complete each of the eight columns, no worries. Fill out as much as you can.):

- Household bills (mortgage or rent, electric and gas, water, insurance, homeowners association, etc.)
- Medical and dental (doctor bills, prescriptions)\
- Child care / Daycare (if you receive a bill)
- Car Payments and other Car Expenses (insurance, gas, maintenance, monthly parking)
- IRS, back-taxes, student loans
- School tuition (if you send your children to private schools or if you or a child are in college)
- Other household utilities (phone, cell phone, cable television, internet)
- Life Insurance Premiums
- Credit Cards
- Collection accounts

As you finish recording each stack – move those bills into a separate file or folder, and label the file with a marker (or at least bundle it together with a rubber band).

And, as a reminder, continue to give yourself those "gold stamps" I talked about every step of the way. Be proud of yourself for taking action!

When you are finished, you should have a list of every single bill that you receive each month, through the mail.

Next, we need to add in some additional monthly expenses. (Later, we'll be adding the bills that aren't billed monthly, such as car licenses, driver's license renewal, memberships, etc., but for right now – we will stay focused here.)

We need to get an estimate (for now, later you'll know exact amounts) of what you're spending on other items that you are currently charging on your credit cards, or other bills that you don't receive a statement for in the mail or by email (If you do charge these expenditures – look at your credit card statements to fill in the totals. Or, if you have been using your debit card to pay these expenses, look at your bank statement.).

List what you spend each month (in the column titled "minimum monthly payments") on:

- Child Support / Alimony (if applicable)
- <u>Essential</u> food and clothing
- Child Care / Day Care
- Gasoline
- Parking
- Public transportation (train/bus)
- Other medical and dental bills

- Life Insurance
- School tuition
- Loans from family and/or friends
- Church or other tithing
- Charitable donations
- Personal Appointments (haircuts, manicures and pedicures, etc.)
- Entertainment (movies, sporting events, etc.)
- Eating out (fast food and sit-down restaurants)
- Other (anything else you spend money on)

If you don't know the exact amount, that's not a problem. Just fill in a rough estimate (for now) of the amount you are spending each month for these expenses.

Next, we need to address the bills that aren't paid each month. I like to call them "non-monthly" bills. These are things such as license tabs, drivers licenses, memberships, etc., that can put a kink in your monthly expenditures if you haven't planned for them. For now, we're going to focus on recording them on the list (on the "Financial Freedom Worksheet," it will automatically add these up and calculate a monthly total).

Click on the tab of "non-monthly" expenses, or on another sheet of paper, fill in estimates (or actual figures, if you know them) for:

- car license tabs
- driver's license renewal
- insurance premiums (if paid annually, or twice per year)
- professional licenses
- memberships
- property taxes (if not escrowed)

Include anything on this list that is not paid regularly.

Now, it's time to "face the music." Take a deep breath and another sip of your favorite beverage because next we're going to calculate how much you are spending each month. No whining, no pity parties. Remember, you're taking control of your financial life, so keep marching on.

Add up the entire "minimum monthly payment" column to get your total monthly expenses. (On the "Financial Freedom Worksheet," the total will be automatically calculated for you.)

Are you surprised at the total? Did you know you were spending so much?

I will be reminding you over and over again of the importance of not beating yourself up at this point – be proud of yourself for choosing to change. Give yourself more imaginary gold stamps.

Okay – now for the "reality check." I'm sure you know this, but we will be focusing on this so much that it's worth discussing. The amount of money you have left at the end of the month is equal to your income minus your expenses.

Money left at the end of the month = Income - Expenses

I'm guessing you already know that this is a negative number right now (otherwise you probably wouldn't have so many debts), but a critical part of our plan will be calculating exactly where you're at.

On a separate sheet of paper (see the separate tab on the "Financial Freedom Worksheet") make a list of your monthly income. Here's how you map out the columns:

Column One: Income Source

Column Two: Date You Are Paid

Column Three: Gross Pay

Column Four: Net Pay

Let's look at what you earned *last* month. List all sources of income from your full-time job, part-time job, side-jobs, home-based businesses, alimony/spousal maintenance, child support, social security, pension – any payment that you receive each month and you can count on.

Now – it's time for "truth telling" about your finances. Pick-up your calculator and start with your income. Add the amount in the "net pay" column to get a grand total of your monthly net income. This is the amount you that comes in your paycheck – that you can save, or use to pay bills.

On a separate sheet of paper – write the magic formula:

Money left at the end of the month = Income - Expenses

Be brave – plug in the numbers. You can't change your finances if you don't know where you're starting. (This will be automatically calculated on the Financial Freedom Worksheet.)

I'm going to take an educated guess that when you take your income, and subtract your expenses – you're coming up with a negative number. Okay – now we have your starting point. Excellent!

Take a couple sips of your favorite beverage – and keep going!

Step Seven: Prioritizing the List

This section may be the most important when it comes to getting rid of some of the stress. It's the question I always wanted to ask all of the experts whose books I devoured.

If I'm not making enough money to cover my bills, how do I figure out what to pay first?

One of the biggest problems I always had implementing my Financial Freedom Strategy was to juggle things while I worked out solutions. And worse yet, I'd get on the phone with a creditor and make promises that were impossible for me to keep.

To avoid that scenario, we're going to put your bills in priority order. (We'll be addressing how to get to "break even" in the next section, but right now we have to help you start "treading water" while we work to fix the rest of your financial issues.)

I'm going to be giving you my viewpoint, and I'm going to share how I personally prioritized the order in which I paid my bills. You might disagree, and that's OK. What's important is that you are using, what money you have right now, to serve you the best it can.

In order to start the discussion of prioritizing your bills, we need to talk about a guy named Maslow.

Abraham Maslow was a psychologist whose theories have been influential during the 20th century. He believed we all have a "hierarchy of needs" beginning with 1) basic needs for food and shelter; 2) needs for safety and security; 3) needs for love and belonging; 4) need for self-esteem; and finally 5) need for self-actualization. We cannot meet the higher needs until the lower ones are met.

The chart on the following page shows the theory:

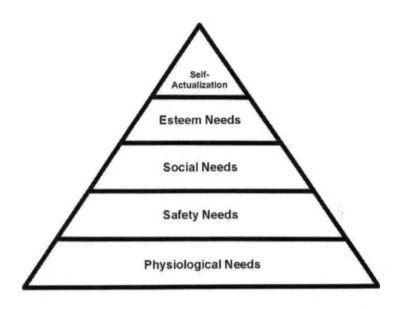

Maslow's Hierarchy of Needs chart

I know, you're wondering where I'm going with this. Here's the thing. Right now, when you are dealing with an overwhelming mountain of debt, the first bills you need to focus on are those that provide food, clothing and shelter (i.e. your physiological needs). That would be your mortgage or rent, essential utilities such as gas and electric, your monthly grocery bills, prescriptions or medical bills, and clothing expenses that are a strict necessity (like your kid who has outgrown his tennis shoes, or needing new undies because all of the elastic has given out on the old ones, but that's about it).

Considering Maslow's hierarchy, I have taken the liberty of labeling each bill on the Financial Freedom Spreadsheet with a priority, with 1 being most important. If you are using your own paper, in the column labeled "priority" put a #1 next to the money you will <u>save</u> each month (for security!), and any bill that deals with household expenses that are an absolute necessity, food that is a necessity (such as groceries), medical expenses (health insurance, prescriptions), and clothing (that is a necessity).

The other payments (if you have this one) that get top priority are child support (this covers the "physiological needs, etc., for your kids) and spousal maintenance (I know, you might really despise giving checks to your ex, but that's not what we need to discuss
here. It's a payment that you are obligated to pay, as determined by the courts, so it goes on the list.)

Now – add up these bills so you can compare this total to your monthly income:

You can cover your family's basic needs (food, clothing, medicine, and shelter) if:

Monthly income IS GREATER THAN THE TOTAL OF "Priority 1" bills

Do this simple calculation:

Total monthly income - "Priority 1" bills = _____

Hopefully this is a nice big, positive number. This should give you the confidence that right now, you are capable of taking care of you and your family's basic needs. If all else fails, you will eat, you will have a roof over your head, and you can get your prescriptions filled.

But what if this number is negative? What if, when you do this calculation, you realize that right now you aren't earning enough money to cover even your most basic needs?

This calls for urgent measures. For now, finish sorting your bills and making the list. Stay focused on the task at hand. We'll be discussing what to do to change these circumstances in the next section.

As we continue to prioritize your bills, and to make decisions about what gets paid and what does not get paid (for now), we will be focusing on a really important number, **remaining available funds (column four).**

Each time we determine that a bill is next in line to get paid, we will subtract it from your monthly income to come up with your **remaining available funds.** We need to monitor this number closely to figure out what you are able to pay each month until you reach the point when you no longer have any money left, <u>at least for now.</u>

The purpose is not to send you off into a worry fest. Rather, we're working to make good decisions with the money you have coming in each month right now.

Prioritizing the rest of your bills

Now that we've addressed your basic needs, it's time to prioritize the rest of your bills – especially if you don't have enough income right now to cover all of them.

Obviously determining which bill takes priority over another – especially when you don't have enough money to cover them all – is a highly personal thing.

I'm not any type of financial advisor (and you may want to consult with one). I'm simply sharing what worked for me. You may not agree (completely) with my evaluation, and that's OK. Our goal is to focus and get you out of this mess as quickly as possible, so please don't get "hung up" at this step by choosing to debate my recommendations. Just keep moving!

Here's how I chose the priority order. Take another look at Maslow's hierarchy of needs chart:

Maslow's Hierarchy of Needs

Now that we've addressed your physiological needs, the next couple priorities will be determined by safety needs.

Second Priority: Child Care

Priority number two is your daycare costs for your children. Obviously you need to provide quality care for your children while you're at work (again, we'll discuss some ideas on how to vary this payment later).

Write a #2 in the priority column next to your monthly daycare costs. And remember to subtract this expense from the "remaining available funds."

Third Priority: Transportation Costs

Your third priority is transportation costs. What are your monthly costs for your vehicle or public transportation? If you have circumstances where you don't need a vehicle, or you don't have to travel to your job, perhaps your only expense is public transportation. But if you do need to commute to work, you need to account for these expenses.

Put a "3" in the priority column next to your car payment, car insurance, monthly gasoline expense and monthly car maintenance costs, or monthly cost for the bus or train. Obviously it is important to have transportation to your job, so this is third on the list. (And again, subtract your transportation expenses from the "remaining funds available" to continue to monitor how much money you have left to work with.)

Fourth priority: Other medical and dental expenses

What do we have if we don't take care of ourselves? Sure, I've put off getting a new crown on a bad tooth, or stretched out my annual physicals a little farther than annually, but it wasn't a good choice. It was me saying "I'm not worthy of taking care of myself."

I'm not talking plastic surgery, breast implants, or the new smile you always dreamed of (unless your doctor feels these treatments are essential for your well-being). Purchase those services when you can pay for them up-front!

Label these expenses with priority 4, and subtract them from your "remaining funds available" total.

Fifth priority: IRS, back-taxes, and student loan payments

Student loan payments and any outstanding tax bills are ahead of credit card bills and collection accounts. Why? Because they are
debts to the federal government.

The government has the ability to go after the money in many ways, but the good news is that it is also willing to work out various solutions from payment plans to forbearance agreements (meaning discontinuing or reducing payment requirements for a period of time, if you have short-term financial challenges such as job loss).

In the priority column, put a number 5 next to any of these bills on the list.

Special note regarding "remaining available funds":

It's possible (or perhaps I should say "likely") that this number will start to be negative. For now – don't worry about it. Just keep going down the list, recording every single monthly bill and expense, and listing them in priority order.

Sixth Priority: Tuition and Student Loans

If you send your children to private school, or you are earning a degree yourself, you may have tuition payments. There are many options for financial assistance (before acquiring student loans) and every school has specialists to help with students' financial needs. But for now, put a 6 next to the amount you are paying monthly for tuition payments, and as a reminder, subtract the expense from "remaining funds available."

Seventh Priority – Loans from family and friends.

It's a category that I haven't seen covered in many books by the financial experts, but I believe it is an incredibly important one. (Especially since, according to Maslow, socialization comes right after safety.) I believe you should start paying off personal loans from family and friends BEFORE you pay off creditors and accounts in collection.

Whether they slipped you $20 bucks for gas, or you owe them a large chunk, it's time to address these bills for a couple reasons – it's good for your relationship, and you owe them the money.

Figure out a reasonable repayment period, based on the amount of debt, the person's urgency (or lack of urgency) for repayment, and a payment that you can commit to.

Let me give you an example. Let's say Rich Aunt Bertha loaned you $1000. She doesn't have an urgent need for the money, and she isn't expecting interest. Perhaps you can start with a 4-year repayment plan.

$1000 divided by 48 months (4 years) = $20.83 per month.

I don't care that Rich Aunt Bertha doesn't need the money. You will feel much better at the next family picnic when you can hold your head high because you are repaying the debt. And, as you start paying off debts, you can increase your payments to deal with it faster.

Let's say that Not-So-Rich Sister Sally covered the family gift for your parents last Christmas, and you haven't paid her the $100 that was your share (perhaps you shouldn't have committed to participate – but too late now!). Set a goal to pay her in a short amount of time – say $25 for four months. She'll be tickled when she starts receiving payments she didn't expect.

You don't want to mess up your relationships. These people will be in your life long after the creditors go away. Figure out how to start paying them something now. Figure out a reasonable place to start, and label each of those debts with a "7" in the priority column and subtract the expense from "remaining funds available."

Eighth Priority: Other Household Utilities (that are not essential)

Next priority is all of those household bills that aren't required for you and your family's well-being. I'm talking the phone, cell phones, cable television and internet access. In the next section we'll be discussing reducing this expense – but for now, they're priority 8.

Here's the thing: if the service gets interrupted because of late or non-payment, you are throwing away money to get the service reinstated.

Give each one an 8, subtract the expense from "remaining funds available," and go to the next priority.

Priority Nine: Other Monthly Expenses

This is the "stuff" that can really eat up your discretionary income, if you're not careful or not paying attention. This is priority 9 simply because they are all expenses that you could temporarily eliminate, if you are in dire straits.

These probably aren't bills you get in the mail. They are probably found as entries on your credit card bills, or they are things you pay for with cash. Estimate your expenses for payments such as church, haircuts, pedicures, any other personal appointment, entertainment (movies, sporting events, etc.), pet food, eating out – basically anything else you spend money on that hasn't been included in the list yet.

Write it all down – even if it is an expense that you are already telling yourself you can eliminate. Right now we're just collecting data to make our plan.

Label each with a 9, subtract the expenses from "remaining funds available," and move on to the next priority.

Priority Ten: The "Irregular" Category – Expenses That Don't Happen Monthly

Recently I coached an elderly woman named Catherine. She asked me to review her monthly spending, because she couldn't figure out why she never seemed to have any money. Catherine's adult daughter, Dianne, was helping Catherine manage her finances, and she was confident that her mother should have plenty of money left after paying her bills each month.

Catherine and I prepared a "Financial Freedom Worksheet," and it quickly became obvious why she was falling short. Dianne had not considered all of Catherine's expenses that weren't paid with a regular, monthly frequency.

If you've kept copies of receipts or recorded payments in your check register, it's an excellent way to pull out the information about these "irregular" expenses. If you don't have that kind of record, simply estimate the amount of the bill, and the month or months when it is paid.

If you're using the "Financial Freedom Worksheet" you'll find a special worksheet (check the tabs at the bottom) where you can record these expenses.

Once you've created the list, we're going to prorate the amount to a monthly expense. (We do that by adding up the total, and dividing by 12. Your "Financial Freedom Worksheet" will calculate it automatically.)

Here are some examples of "irregular" bills:

- *water bill / garbage bill*
- *car license*
- *driver's license*
- *any other professional license renewal*
- *subscriptions*
- *memberships*
- *summer camp*
- *sporting team fees*
- *fundraisers*
- *renters insurance*

Even if you're not sure what the total amount is of each payment, record an estimate. Now, add the total, divide that number by 12, and make an entry on your "Financial Freedom Worksheet" for this amount, so you plan for it monthly. Title it: "bills that aren't paid monthly." Give the category a priority of 10.

Priority Eleven: Life Insurance Premiums

There are many different types of life insurance. Obviously, if you have a life insurance policy, it is important to you to leave your family with some financial security, should something happen to you. Or perhaps you're using life insurance as an investment tool. Whatever the case may be, it's an expense that you've chosen to pay each month.

Again, the purpose is not to argue about where life insurance ranks in importance – our goal is to get control of your finances.

I gave Life Insurance Premiums an 11 at this point. Remember to subtract the monthly premiums from "remaining available funds."

Priority Twelve: Paying Your Credit Cards.

If you have any remaining money after covering the bills we discussed above (saving an emergency fund; food, clothing, shelter and medicine; child support; alimony; life insurance; daycare; transportation; federal government debts such as taxes and student loans; loans from family and friends) we go to the next category on

the list -- your credit cards.

Hopefully you are earning enough to make your minimum payments, because building and maintaining a good credit rating impacts so many things in your life.

But if you're not making enough to cover them, and you've been doing the "credit card shuffle" (where you take a cash advance from one to make the minimum payments on the others) then that behavior has got to stop.

(If you choose to start a home party or network marketing business - I love coaching my students to choose one of their credit card bills, and make it a goal to earn enough in their business in one month to pay it off completely. It gives them a focus, and makes them realize just how powerful they are to take control of and change their circumstances!)

Credit cards are near the bottom of my priority list for a couple different reasons. Credit card debt is unsecured debt. Credit card companies chose to take a calculated risk when they established the credit for you, but that credit was not backed with any type of collateral, such as a home or a vehicle.

Obviously you created the debt, and you hope to repay the bills. But if you don't have the funds to cover your credit card bills at this time, they are the ones that get put off while you're "in transition" to managing your finances well.

If you have some funds available, but not enough to cover all of the minimum payments, how do you choose which ones to pay?

Look at the portion of your list with unsecured debt and put the list in order from **lowest to highest** minimum monthly payment.

Since you know (from your chart) the amount of money you have left to apply to credit card bills, figure out which ones you are able to pay.

For example, say you have $150 available to pay towards your credit card bills, and you have six credit cards to pay, listed from lowest to highest minimum payment like so:

Credit Card #1: $ 35.00

Credit Card #2: $ 45.00

Credit Card #3: $ 50.00

Credit Card #4:	$ 75.00
Credit Card #5:	$100.00
Credit Card #6:	$110.00

Based on $150, make full minimum monthly payments to credit cards #1-3 ($35, $45, $50 = $130), and pay the remaining balance of $20 to credit card #4. Credit cards # 5 and #6 will have to wait - at least for now, as you continue to develop your plan.

In the next sections, we'll be talking about ways to reduce expenses, and ways to come up with more money (you can do this VERY QUICKLY by starting a home party or network marketing business) – hopefully enough to make full minimum payments to cards #4-6 – but for right now, today, this is the short-term plan to manage what you've got.

Right now, as you work to get a handle on what is coming in and what is going out, the reason for paying your credit cards in this manner is two-fold. It will allow you to spread the remaining money to as many accounts as possible, and, in general the accounts with the lowest balances will probably have the lowest minimum payments. As you start to find more money (which we will be discussing later) you will make major progress by paying off the lowest balance accounts, then rolling that monthly payment to your next balance.

You will get late notices and phone calls (you probably already have) from the credit card companies that aren't getting paid. Let them know that right now you don't have the ability to make the payments.

And this is critically important: **Never make a promise to a creditor that you can't keep.**

The customer service reps who call you are trained to get you to make a commitment. They will try to offer you a great deal if you set-up a payment arrangement with them on the phone (and often they will ask you to post-date a check). **Don't do it!** Politely explain that right now you do not have the resources to make a commitment. Explain that you are working diligently to get your finances under control, and you will be happy to keep them informed as you work to change your circumstances.

One of my relentless creditors tried to bully me by saying "We will be continuing to call you everyday until this is resolved." My response, "You can call me several times a day if you choose. That isn't going to change my circumstances, and frankly, it will be chewing up valuable time that I could be devoting to increasing my income. But you're welcome to call."

Keep your monthly expense chart near the phone so you aren't tempted or bullied into a commitment. Right now, the funds just aren't there.

Remember - your response is that you are sorry, but today you can't make the payment or make a commitment.

And if they persist, hang up the phone. Plain and simple…click.

Write a "12" in the priority column next to the credit card bills that you are able to pay each month (minimum payments). Write a "13" in the priority column next to the credit card bills that you can only pay partially, or not at all.

Last on the List – Priority Thirteen: Collection Accounts.

If you have accounts that have already been sent to collectors, then you have already started to receive the threatening letters and phone calls. Once an account goes to a collection agency, these companies are paid a portion of any amount they recover, which is why they are relentless (and often, unscrupulous).

At this stage, it's important to know your rights. Collection agencies are governed by Fair Debt Collection Practices Act (FDCPA).

I put a pdf of the Act on my website: **BlastAwayYourDebt.com**

Here is a partial list of what they <u>are</u> and <u>are not</u> allowed to do, from the pdf (but I highly encourage you to review the pdf document in its entirety):

- *Debt Collectors may not contact you at inconvenient times or places, such as before 8 a.m. or after 9 p.m., unless you agree to it.*

- *Debt Collectors may not contact you at work if they're told (orally or in writing) that you're not allowed to get calls there.*

- *If you decide you don't want a debt collector to contact you again, tell the collector, in writing, to stop contacting you. Do this by sending a certified letter, with a return receipt. Once they receive your letter they may not contact you again, with two exceptions: they may contact you to tell you there will be no further contact or to let you know that they or the creditor intend to take a specific action, such as filing a lawsuit. (Note: sending such a letter does not get rid of the debt, but it should stop the contact.)*

- *Debt collector must send you a written "validation notice" telling you how much money you owe within five days after they first contact you. This notice must include the name of the creditor to whom you owe the money, and how to proceed if you don't think you owe the money.*

- *Debt collectors may not lie when they are trying to collect a debt.*

- *Debt collectors may not harass, oppress, or abuse you or any third parties they contact. For example, they may not use threats of violence or harm; publish a list of names of people who refuse to pay their debts; use obscene or profane language; or repeatedly use the phone to annoy someone.*

- *If you don't pay a debt, a creditor or its debt collector generally can sue you to collect. If they win, the court will enter a judgment against you. The judgment states the amount of money you owe, and allows the creditor or collector to get a garnishment order against you, directing a third party (like your bank) to turn over funds from your account to pay the debt.*

If you believe a debt collector has violated the law, you have the right to sue a collector in a state or federal court within one year from the date the law was violated. If you win, the judge can require the collector to pay you for any damages you can prove you suffered because of the illegal collection practices, like lost wages and medical bills.

Right now we have to stop the financial bleeding and take control. Collection accounts are last in line. Be firm, and don't hesitate to hang-up the phone.

When I needed to get some relief from their relentless phone calls, I turned off the ringer on my phone. These days you can block their call from your cell phone.

That gave me the choice to return their calls, or delete their messages (which I did most of the time).

Review

Let's do a quick review of where we're at so far.

- You made a commitment that you will not go further into debt today (and you will make that same commitment to yourself every single day).

- You have started saving money for extreme emergencies only – even if it is $5 bucks a week (for now!).

- You opened your mail, sorted it into its appropriate categories, and designated a specific location in the house (in a box or drawer) where you will keep the bills when they arrive.

- You made a commitment to open your mail and review your bills at a regular, scheduled time each week.

- You made a list of your monthly bills, along with the details of each bill.

- You added regular monthly expenses to that list.

- And, you added expenses that don't occur monthly, such as licenses, etc., and prorated them to a monthly expense. You determined if you are earning enough to cover your "basic needs" of food, clothing, child support, medicine and shelter.

- You prioritized the remainder of your bills by numbering them 1-13, and listed your credit cards in order, based on lowest to highest minimum payment. You determined which you are able to pay now – and which have to wait, temporarily.

Didn't it feel great to take action? Even though we have more work to complete, I know you are feeling good already, even if the picture has been a bit bleak. You are on the path to financial freedom. Obviously you really want this, so roll up your sleeves. We have more work to do.

Now we have to focus on two specific areas. Remember our formula?

Money left at the end of the month = income – expenses

The next two sections deal with the two things that can have an immediate impact on your financial life – your expenses and your income.

Step Eight: Spend Less

You've done a great job so far. So now it's time to get brutal.

At this stage in our "take control of your finances" plan, we're going to scrutinize your expenses. We are going to see where we can squeeze money out of the money that you are currently making. Think of it like a damp towel. Although it may just feel damp, when you twist it and wring it, you can squeeze some more water out of it. We're going to do the exact same thing with your finances.

Right now, look at the column marked **remaining available funds** on your spreadsheet. Did you complete the calculation all the way to the bottom of the chart, even if it was a negative number (and I'd be surprised if it wasn't a negative number, so no worries).

Our first goal is to figure out how to get you to Break Even.

Let's say, for example, that you completed the chart and found that if you paid every single monthly bill on the list, you are $450 short each month (in other words, the balance at the bottom of your "remaining available funds" column is -$450.00). That means to get to break even -- the point where the amount you earn is <u>equal</u> to the amount you spend -- we have to figure out how to either eliminate $450 worth of expense, or generate an additional $450 in income, or do a combination of the two (meaning, as an example, decrease your expenses by $250 AND increase your income by $200, for a total of $450).

Getting to break even is the ONLY way to stop digging your financial hole deeper.

We're going to focus on reducing expenses first.

You can make an immediate impact on your finances – TODAY – by eliminating or reducing expenses. So right now, we're going to scrutinize every entry on your list to determine what expense you can reduce and what expense you can eliminate completely.

Again - I'm not a financial advisor or an accountant. My purpose is to give you ideas for ways you can reduce your expenses. In some cases, you may need to seek out professional advice before making any changes.

Label the remaining two columns on your spreadsheet (these are already included on the "Financial Freedom Worksheet," as follows:

Column 9 – amount expense is reduced

Column 10 – remaining amount to get to break even

In column 9, you will record the amount that you have "squeezed out" of your monthly expenses, and in column 10 you will monitor (by subtracting) how much money you have to continue to "find" (either through expense reduction or additional income) to get to *break even*.

So let's start going down the list, one category at a time.

We'll start by discussing your housing expenses (obviously you can work to reduce your food and clothing expense – and we'll get there later -- but housing expenses is the area where most people can make a dramatic impact the fastest).

Let me tell you about Ben and Marcy, a couple who lived across the street from me. They were getting ready to start a family, and they realized that they were living in a home that would soon be too expensive for their budget, once they added the costs of a new addition to the family. They tried to sell the property, but with declining prices in the real estate market at the time, they could not get any offers close to their asking price.

This resourceful couple tapped into their resources. They moved in with relatives and rented out their town home. I have no idea what kind of relationship they have with their family. I'm sure, at times it isn't easy to live in your parents' basement. But at the same time, this gave Ben and Marcy the opportunity to save money to eventually build or buy a single family residence, while taking good care of their credit with on-time mortgage payments.

If you are behind on your mortgage payment, believe it or not, there are lots of options available to you, but you must take <u>immediate action.</u>

The first call should be to your local housing assistance program (probably through your county). Explain your situation, ask them what options are available, and ask for their advice.

You may be able to qualify for a mortgage loan modification. This would be a way to reduce your mortgage interest and monthly payments, as a result of your lender modifying the details of your current home loan. This is not refinancing. This is better than refinancing for the most part, because there will be a lot of fees involved in refinancing (often anywhere from 2-4% of the loan amount), versus possibly a very small processing fee from your lender for a modification.

Loan modification programs are offered through your current lender. They will ask you for a lot of financial documentation (copies of your monthly pay stubs, bank statements, past two years of taxes, and a review of your monthly bills – similar to the list you just prepared) to determine your qualifications for a modification. If approved, the result can be a reduction in your monthly payments, your interest rate, even your remaining mortgage balance.

Getting a mortgage loan modification may take a lot of work and a lot of phone calls, but it can be worth the energy and time if it helps you reduce your monthly housing expense.

And, if you're in "deep kaka" – you may need to consider a short sale of your home. This means that you put your home on the market and, if you receive and choose to accept an offer that is less than what you owe on the property, you work with your lender to ask them to absorb the loss, rather than you needing to bring money to the closing table.

Many real estate salespeople are highly experienced in short sales and can guide you through the process, so I strongly recommend that you get professional assistance if you choose this route to reduce your housing expense.

People often cringe at the thought of selling their home. It's just a house. It's constructed of concrete, studs, drywall, roofing material, etc., and it can be replaced when you are in a financial position that allows you to easily afford the payments.

The problem is, people get emotionally attached to their house. It's where their first baby was born, or it has the kitchen they always dreamed of, or it has been in the family for a couple generations.

None of those things matter when you can't afford the payments. What matters is that you take action to get yourself out from under the payments, and into something you can afford. This will be much better for you for years to come, rather than the damage you will do to yourself financially by making late payments or

allowing your home to go into foreclosure. In my opinion, you must avoid foreclosure at all costs (and remember, I'm speaking from experience here)!

What about renters?

If you are renting, and you can't currently afford your monthly rent payments, you have a much easier solution – move! Start by talking to your current landlord to explain your situation. He or she may have options to move you to a less expensive unit in the same complex, or with some of the big management companies, they may be willing to help you move into a different property that charges lower rent. If you've been a good tenant, hopefully they will work with you to find some solutions (and if you've been a pain in the (you know what), they probably won't be very helpful!).

There are some costs involved with moving, such as packing boxes, renting a truck, buying beer for all of your friends who agree to help, utility hook-ups, security deposits, etc., so evaluate this carefully. I also recommend that you get approved in a new unit before turning in your notice (just like it's easier to look for a new job
when you are employed).

Also, if you are trying to move before your lease is up, your current management company may ask you to try to sublet your rental unit (put an ad on Craig's list for free!), and they will require that a new tenant be screened through their approval process. But if they are a decent landlord, they will prefer that you are honest and up-front about your circumstances, and will work with you to find a solution.

We've covered some ideas for taking control of your monthly housing expenses. Now let me share a great idea that helped me take control of my costs and have financial confidence for the other "basic needs" – food, gasoline, and clothing. I call it the "gift card" technique.

The "Gift-Card" Technique

We've talked about the importance of starting to save money immediately. I also want to share a concept that really helped me as I was rebuilding my financial life, and that is using gift cards. This is a way to start pre-paying for groceries, gas, medicine and other basic living expenses out of each paycheck. It's also a great way to keep these expenses within your budget (yikes, did I just say that word – "budget?" Yes, that is basically what we've been working on.)

As usual, I figured out the "gift card technique" when I found myself in dire straits. At the time, I was paid every two weeks. My gas tank was down to fumes, and I was flat broke (didn't even have pennies left to cash-in at the grocery store). I needed to cover my expenses to get to work for the next week until payday.

Fortunately, a dear friend floated me $20 bucks until payday. I was totally embarrassed that I had to ask, and that day I vowed that I would never find myself with an empty tank again. That's when I came up with the *gift card technique.*

Here's how it works: when you get your paycheck, you first take out and tuck away savings (or even better, have them automatically deposited to a savings account from your paycheck); then you stop at the grocery store to purchase a gift card that will cover your grocery expenses until your next check. Next, go to the gas station and do the same thing. And third, if you have prescriptions that need filling, purchase a gift card at the pharmacy. Make sure that you ask for gift cards that can be "re-charged" each month and use cards that do not expire.

When your tank is empty, you can swing into the gas station with confidence because you've got the funds available on your gift card.

Need some milk? Same thing. Buzz into the grocery store with your gift card in-hand to make your purchase.

Time to get a prescription refilled? You've got the payment covered already.

You will be amazed how this small activity with each paycheck can start to build your financial confidence. And, when you know what is available on the card, it will make you think carefully about how you spend those dollars. You'll start to ask yourself, do I *need* it, or do I just *want* it?

This is another concept that deserves some discussion.

Do you NEED it or do you just WANT it?

As we review a list of ideas for reducing expenses, I want you to think of the concept of "need versus want." Let me give you an example. Let's say that you have the deluxe package of cable television that includes all of the movie channels and all of the sports channels – you name it, you have it. Although you may choose to argue with me, I would claim that this is a *want*, rather than a *need*. How much money can you save if you cut back to basic service, or better yet, eliminate cable all together?

What follows is a list of ideas of expenses that I believe you can reduce or eliminate because they are "wants" – not "needs." I'll share some of the expenses I cut out myself, and I know you will also come up with many of your own. For now, the goal is to reduce enough expenses to get to **break even**, where

Income = expenses

Won't that feel great??

Let's continue to review the rest of the categories on the "Financial Freedom Worksheet." As you reduce an expense, make sure you record the amount in column 9 "amount expense is reduced" and keep a running balance in Column 10 "remaining amount to get to break even" so you can see your progress. As you go through this process, keep asking yourself, "Is this a *want* or is this a *need?*"

Additional expenses you can eliminate:

Mortgage or Rent – as we discussed above, work on a loan modification, sell your house, or, if renting, work with your property management company to move to a less expense rental unit.

(When life imploded, I lost my home to foreclosure – bad move! While I was getting back on track, I rented my friend's basement for $500 per month. Had I rented an apartment, my expense would have been $800 to $900 per month plus utilities, so this saved me about $600 per month.)

Electric and Gas – it's time to learn to conserve. Shut off lights when you leave a room; turn the setting on your thermostat down in the winter, and turn it up in the summer; unplug your electronics; switch to energy efficient light bulbs; and call your utility company immediately to get on a "budget plan."

I can reduce this expense by: _____ per month

Water: Do you wash large loads of laundry? Do you waste water? I became more cognizant of the amount of water I was using. Although this expense reduction may not seem like a lot, when you're in survival mode, every dollar is important, and takes you one step closer to *break even.*

I can reduce this expense by: _____ per month

<u>Renter's or Homeowner's Insurance:</u> I was living in a townhome, so my unit was insured against fire or storm loss and liability by the homeowner's association. I also do not have expensive jewelry or artwork. Probably my only assets are computers. So…I dropped my renter's insurance** (which covered my belongings) to reduce expenses. My annual premium was $145.

I can reduce this expense by: _____ per month

**Be sure to review this carefully with your insurance professional. I didn't have any expensive belongings that needed coverage. Make it clear to your agent that for now, you have to reduce your expenses, and find out what they can suggest to help you accomplish that goal.

<u>Property Taxes</u>: If you own your home, you may consider talking to your county about reducing your property taxes – especially if you're in an area where home values have plummeted. Call your county to get more information. If your property taxes are escrowed into your mortgage payment, you will also need to provide proof of this reduction to your lender, and it could take a few months before you see the reduction in your escrow payment.

I can reduce this expense by: _____ per month

Home Phone (i.e. "land line")

I eliminated my home phone all together, especially since I have a cell phone. Ask yourself how often you actually use this line, and if you don't have a *need* for it, get rid of it. Susie's monthly savings: $62.35

I can reduce this expense by: _____ per month

Cell Phone

It seems that cell phone companies change their plans about as often as you change a baby's diaper. Evaluate your family's cell phone needs carefully, and start shopping for a new plan. (Or better yet – can you eliminate cell phones for now?) It's amazing what cell phone companies will offer when you threaten to move your service! If you change plans, make sure your children are well-aware of the "new rules" on cell phone use so you don't end up with a huge "over your minutes" or texting bill (and monitor the minutes throughout the month to make sure it doesn't happen!).

I can reduce this expense by: _____ per month

Cable Television and Internet

Get rid of it! I know, you'll argue that you *need* these things desperately. Unless you have a business that requires internet access, you will be just fine without either of these services. I put my television in storage, and started going to the library with my laptop to access the internet. (The library also has computers available, if you don't have a laptop) If you can't completely wean yourself, at least reduce your services. You don't need all the movie channels, or the extended package for that matter.

I can reduce this expense by: _____ per month

Daycare

Let me confess – I don't have children. I never met the man who deserved me (or, as my friends would tell you, I never met the

man who would put up with me), so for me to give any type of recommendations about Daycare would be, in my opinion, hypocritical.

Obviously if you work, you need to provide excellent care for your children, and I'm confident you have a list of criteria that are very important to you when choosing a daycare provider.

Some ideas to consider as you evaluate your expense in this category:

- While you work to get your finances back on track, do you have a relative or friend who could provide daycare for a limited period of time (such as two-to-three months)?

- Can you arrange any type of "child-care trade" – meaning a friend cares for your children while you work, and you care for the friend's children evenings and/or weekends?

- Can you rearrange your work hours so one parent works days, then cares for your children in the evening, while the other parent works evenings, then cares for the children during the day? (And this can work, even if you're divorced or separated!)

As I said, I'm just throwing out some ideas for you to consider as ways to reduce your costs. Children are precious and they are our future, and I'm confident you'll make a decision that considers their well-being first.

I can reduce this expense by: _____ per month

Child Support and Spousal Maintenance

Remember, I don't have children and I don't have an "ex" (at least not one that I was married to). I'm going to share my opinion, which you may or may not agree with, and that's OK.

First, I can't imagine any parent that doesn't want to take good care of their children. For purposes of taking control of your finances, it doesn't matter if you don't like how your "ex" manages the child support payment. It's an obligation that you have, so put it on the list. Spending even one moment wasting energy on how the money is used does not serve our bigger purpose here, so move on.

As far as spousal maintenance goes, depending on your relationship with your "ex," perhaps you can negotiate a lower payment while you get back on track (or perhaps that's not an option). Yes, you may be able to go back to the courthouse, but wouldn't it be more powerful to spend that energy on moving to financial freedom? Do you really want to take on additional attorney costs right now?

Make a good decision, and take action.

I can reduce this expense by: _____ per month

Life Insurance

If you have a life insurance policy, whether you can reduce the amount of your monthly payment really depends on a few factors.

First, talk to your insurance agent.

Do you have term or whole life? Term insurance is strictly a policy that will pay your heirs a sum of money, in the event of your death. Whole life insurance is an account that builds up a cash value, and has more options – but because it has options, it is also more expensive.

While you are working to get your finances back on track, you may want to find ways to keep the coverage that you need, while decreasing your monthly expense by changing policy type. Again, review this carefully with a professional.

Amount of monthly expense reduction: _____

Medical and Dental Insurance

This is an area where you have to make some careful decisions – and, as much as this will sound like I am contradicting myself, it may be an area where you do not eliminate any expenses. I have been blessed with excellent health, so I didn't have a lot of expense in the medical category. At the same time, I was also "blessed" with crappy teeth, and that is an area where I couldn't reduce any expenses. Evaluate this area carefully, and don't feel bad if there is nothing you can eliminate.

Consider switching to generic medications (with the approval of your doctor). Depending on your health insurance plan, and how often you go to the doctor, you may be able to reduce a health insurance premium by increasing your deductible, but again, evaluate this decision very carefully based on you and your family's circumstances.

I can reduce this expense by: _____ per month

Transportation (Car expenses, gasoline, public transportation)

First, let me tell you my car story.

This is another lesson I learned the hard way. For several years in a row, I traded vehicles every couple years. I would drive them to the point where they were going to start needing some major "preventive maintenance" costs, and then I would trot into the dealer and negotiate a trade. Since I was "upside down" meaning I owed more on the vehicle than it was worth, the dealers would happily roll the difference into my new car loan at outrageous interest rates.

I didn't care. All I cared about was getting a new vehicle. And worse, I bought new, rather than used. Each time I traded, my payments would go higher and higher, to the point where I was paying $827.00 per month for my car payment. That's a mortgage payment – for a car. How ridiculous!

I was already struggling to make the payments, when the women's clothing company that I had been affiliated with for 19 years ceased operations. It wasn't a surprise – it had been dying a "slow and painful death" for about seven years – but at the same time, it meant that my income also ceased (with that company "owing me" about $6000 in unpaid commissions). As a self-employed person, I also didn't qualify for unemployment.

Needless to say, I wasn't able to make my car payments.

I started applying for jobs at the worst possible time, but, after taking most of my background and qualifications off my resume, I was hired in a high-level administrative assistant position for a local newspaper (after four months of having no income, and no savings to tap into).

I knew there was an "active repossession" on my car – but I really didn't pay attention to what that meant. I was in contact with my loan company, and I had notified them of my new job. But I wasn't able to catch up the payments at this point.

My fourth week on the job, I went to work early one morning to complete a project. I parked my car on the street, and planned to move it into the parking lot during the "daily special" parking times (which meant paying $7.00 per day, rather than $16.00).

I walked out of the building, with my keys in-hand, only to find that my car was missing-in-action.

The repo guys had probably followed me from my house to work, and towed it right off the street after I parked and walked into the building.

And, to make matters worse, after they sold the car at the auction, the loan company sent me a bill for the difference between what was owed versus what it sold for – to the tune of about $24,000.

Stuck without a vehicle, I now learned about public transportation. The nearest bus-stop was about two-and-a-half miles from my home, so I was getting up and out the door at 5 a.m. in order to arrive at my new job on time (at 8 a.m.).   And, I live in Minnesota.   This happened as winter was approaching, so I was also bundling up with clothes several layers thick, to keep warm during my trek to the bus stop.

Another hard lesson I have learned is when you put yourself in desperate situations, let me be blunt – you get screwed. (Sorry if that term offends you - but there is no better description.

I needed some sort of vehicle, but obviously I was not able to qualify for conventional financing, so I went to one of the local "sharks" to buy a car.

This experience was certainly an interesting lesson in sales. Here's how it went:

First, they collected all of my financial information and pulled my credit.

Next, reciting a well-rehearsed script, the salesperson started with the "sales 101" questions, while a co-worker went out to bring up the car that they felt I could afford:

"Right now you need a vehicle, don't you?"

"If we can help you improve your credit by reporting your on-time payments, that will be a benefit to you, won't it?"

And my personal favorite statement:

"We are here to help."

They had testimonials and photos of "happy customers" plastered on the walls like wallpaper (note: they pay a $100 bonus to people who give them a testimonial).

Next, they send you off to test-drive your new vehicle. In my case, this was a 4-door something that looked like it had been in a gang-war. The dashboard had been burned and the plastic was melted. So much air blew through the doors that there was no need for a fan. And the lock on the driver's side door no longer worked.

Never once did the company tell me what they were charging for the vehicle. They strictly based the car they provided on the payments that I could afford.

I made the decision to walk. I said "Thank you for your willingness to help me," and started out the parking lot towards the bus stop.

That's when the manager chased me down. She said, "Look – you need a car – you have a repo, and your credit is in the trash – so what's the deal."

I politely explained that as much as I needed a car, I felt the vehicle they showed me would quickly require major repair expenses – something I couldn't afford at the time.

The manager said that for a couple extra dollars per paycheck (again, not telling me a price) she could get me into a different vehicle. She proceeded to scrape the snow off of the vehicle I eventually named "Bessy," a 1997 Mitsubishi Galant with 100,000 miles on it.

Like I said, desperate people do desperate things, so I proceeded with the purchase. To complete the deal they make you watch their "customer video" that walks you through the stack of documents that you'll sign – I'm sure carefully crafted by an attorney to cover their butts legally. Next, they ask you to enter the name and phone number of **12 references** into their computer system. (Can you believe it – 12 references??) And finally, after setting up the payments to automatically come out of each paycheck, they congratulate you and hand you the keys to your vehicle.

Later that night, I looked up the blue book value of Bessy. According to the paperwork, I was charged $7095 for this car. Blue book was about $1600. My interest rate was 19.99% (probably a level just under the limit of the usury laws).

Let me say it again: desperate people do desperate things. The best way to not get screwed is by NOT being desperate. When you take control of your finances, you put yourself in the driver's seat, rather than being at the mercy of these sharks.

If you need a different vehicle, buy a used one. And, if at all possible, buy from a private individual, negotiate a fair, but good deal, and have a mechanic check out the car before completing the purchase. And, from now on, **pay cash!**

Whew – OK – back to expenses you can reduce or eliminate in this category:

Car Payments:

Can you reduce or eliminate this payment, either by "trading down" to a less expensive car, selling a car, or working with your lender to reduce your monthly payment? I can reduce this expense by: _____ per month

Car Insurance

Either shop for new insurance, or decrease your monthly payments by increasing your deductible.

Susie's monthly savings: $0 (I always had a high deductible, and decent rates. I did shop around, but for me, this wasn't an area where I found any savings. I do want to encourage you to review this carefully – I've heard of reductions of anywhere from $25 to $75 per month!)

I can reduce this expense by: _____ per month

Gasoline

It's time to start getting anal about your driving. Can you carpool to work? Can you organize your errands for efficiency? And can you talk to other parents about sharing driving responsibilities? Using the "gas card technique" is also a great way to put you and your family on a "gasoline budget" – when your gift card is empty, no more gasoline until next payday.

Hopefully you also have considered your gasoline expense when you traded or purchased vehicles. If you are a multi-car family, drive the car that gets the best gas mileage (and consider selling or, at least parking, the other one!).

I can reduce this expense by: _____ per month

Car Maintenance

Be careful with this one. I'm a big believer in "preventive maintenance" mainly because if you don't take good care of your vehicle, you'll probably end up with higher repair costs when things breakdown. (And paying for a tow truck isn't cheap, either.)

Perhaps you can stretch a little – go a little further between oil changes, or do some comparison shopping for rates at repair shops, but don't create a bigger expense by eliminating regular maintenance.

I can reduce this expense by: _____ per month

Public Transportation

If you are able to use a bus or train, great! No need to keep a car. You can reduce some of your costs by purchasing passes. Contact your local transit company for more details. (You may be able to save $10 to $30 per month, depending on your frequency and distance traveled.)

I can reduce this expense by: _____ per month

Parking and commuting expenses

I started a job in downtown St. Paul, and that meant I had to pay for parking. If I parked in the lot near my office, the charge was $7.50 per day, or $140 per month on a contract. I found a lot about eight blocks from the building where the charge was $1.50 per day. I got great exercise by parking Bessy "in the back forty," as I called it, and saved about $110 per month on parking fees. Can you reduce your commuting expense? Maybe you can find a way to carpool, or find a way to work from home, at least some days each week.

I can reduce this expense by: _____ per month

Reminder: Keep recording the amount that you reduce each expense by, to figure out when you reach "break even." And if you are already at *break even* or better yet – you have money left over after paying the minimum payments on all of your bills and regular expenses – don't stop! Keep going to see how much money you can free up! You might get out of debt faster than you think!

Debts to the IRS, State or County (a.k.a. back taxes)

Depending on the mess that you have with the IRS (meaning the amount of the back taxes that you owe, perhaps liens and levies, etc.), you may need to consult with a professional.

Here's what I recommend on this topic. Whether you choose to work out a solution with the IRS on your own, or you consult with a professional, start taking action immediately. Based on what I've learned by attending a couple seminars and reading a couple great

books on the topic, this doesn't necessarily mean that you contact the IRS. There may different strategies depending on the status of your past-due taxes, including how long ago you obtained the debt. The one thing to consider: The longer delay figuring out a plan and taking action, the worse it will get. And, the longer you delay, the bigger the bill (with interest and penalties).

Even if you can't pay immediately or need to work out a payment plan, offer-in-compromise, or some other solution, you absolutely must file your taxes.

If you do choose to work with an attorney or accountant, check them out carefully before you hire their services. That means asking for references, ask how many cases they have successfully negotiated with the IRS, and call those people for verification. If they aren't willing to give you any references, then they aren't the right company for you to work with.

I hired the wrong attorney to help me with my tax debt. All he did was "regurgitate" the forms and financials that I filled out. More than $2500 later, he not only didn't make any progress with the IRS, on my behalf, he actually made matters worse. I eventually met with the IRS on my own.

There are several companies, who spend a lot of money advertising, or putting on "free seminars" at the local hotel, that will happily take on your IRS problems, with the claim, "We'll settle your case for pennies on the dollar." Again, be careful! That's all I have to say about that.

If you are experiencing financial hardship, and you are already on a payment plan with the IRS, contact to negotiate a lower payment. Again, do your homework.

Not dealing with my IRS bill cost me dearly – in stress, in worry-time, and in dollars. So if this is also true for you, just for today, continue working through this assignment. Tomorrow, dealing with your taxes that are owed must go to the top of your "financial-to-do" list.

It's also time to deal with other past-due taxes, such as state income tax or delinquent property taxes.

After you complete this financial management plan, you will have all the information to work out a payment plan with your state (and do complete the plan first, because you'll know exactly how much you can commit to for a monthly payment).

Delinquent property taxes are a beast. Here's the scary part, depending on the state where you live. Property taxes go into "first lien position" meaning counties can supersede your mortgage when it comes to taking your property. In some states, counties can even issue "tax lien certificates" which they sell to investors (this is a way for the county to get the cash they need, that they haven't been able to collect form you). Not to bore you with all the legalities, but what is important is that this is not a debt to be ignored. Again, once you have finished this "Financial Freedom Plan," you'll know how much cash you have available to work out a payment plan with your county, if you are behind on any property taxes.

I can reduce this expense by: _____ per month

Student Loans

The challenge on student loans is that, like taxes, they are government backed loan programs. That means they can reach much further into your financial life than other types of creditors by seizing tax refunds, garnishing your wages, and much more.

After I took control of my finances, I called my student loan processor and requested a forbearance on my account. For a period of one year, they allowed me to discontinue the payments (keep in mind that interest continues to add to the balance during this period). Then, they granted an additional forbearance for another year for a reduced payment ($100 versus $138.79). My goal was to free up this money to get to break even. Since my student loan was at a much lower interest rate than my credit cards (6% versus anywhere from 19.99% to 29.99%!), I used that additional amount ($38.79) to pay off more costly debt.

I can reduce this expense by: _____ per month

Tuition

Perhaps you have tuition payments for yourself, your college-age children, or young children that you have enrolled in private school.

If you're in school – good for you! Especially if it will help you increase your income by meeting the qualifications of jobs that have higher pay.

The biggest thing I want to encourage you to do for all tuition payments is to check out scholarships and grants. Call the financial aid department at each school and ask for help. There is lots of money out there for students (at all levels of education). You just have to be willing to work through lots of red tape to find and apply for the programs.

Loans from Family and Friends

First, let me give you my two cents about borrowing from family members or friends. DON'T DO IT!

You know the saying, "hindsight is 20:20" – and I can tell you that despite all of the other financial mistakes that I made in my life, borrowing money from family members and friends was the worst mistake I made.

From my experience, you will do long-term damage if you do this.

I explained how to put payments for loans in your financial plan. So if you like my advice, you may take a step backwards in this category. If you haven't been making payments on those loans, start now!

I can reduce this expense by: _____ per month

Credit Cards

Earlier I explained how to put your credit cards in order from lowest balance to highest balance (and hopefully lowest monthly payment to highest monthly payment).

Look at each of your credit card statements carefully. I recommend that you add one more column to your *"Financial Freedom" worksheet* titled "<u>percent</u> minimum monthly payment" (again, if you downloaded the excel spreadsheet from the website at BlastAwayYourDebt.com, it is there, and calculated for you already).

The reason this is important is to determine if you can transfer any balances without going backwards on your minimum monthly payments.

Right now you are drowning in debt. Right now you aren't making enough money to cover your monthly finances. Read this carefully: if you transfer a balance to a lower interest account that has a higher percent minimum monthly payment, your monthly payment will probably increase rather than decrease. Right now, until you get your finances under control, you can't handle that increase in your monthly payment.

Later, as you have more control of your finances, transferring balances is *possibly* a good move. But right now, our focus is to reduce your monthly payments.

Although it is often recommended by financial experts, I never had much luck with negotiating a lower interest rate on my credit cards. It doesn't mean you can't try it; I'm just telling you that I personally never had any success.

The biggest immediate impact you can have in this category is to commit to the following:

1) Stop charging on these cards – NOW! Put them away in a sealed envelope, or do the old "submerse them in a can of water, and freeze it" routine so it would take a day of thawing to get at the card.

Whatever it takes, make a commitment NOW that you absolutely will not charge one additional item.

2) Pay the minimum payment <u>on time</u> so you don't have any additional late fees adding to your balance.

Again, we'll be doing more in this category once you are above water, but right now you'll be paying them in order from lowest minimum monthly payment to highest.

Here's what you should <u>NOT</u> do right now – and that is <u>DO NOT close any of your credit card accounts</u>. This can have a negative impact on your credit score. For now, our focus is to get you "floating" financially, rather than drowning. Keep going.

Collection Accounts

Whether you have unpaid medical bills or other debts that have gone to collection agencies, these are the "ugly beasts." When collection agencies take-on these accounts, they are paid a portion of what they collect. It's no wonder they are relentless, and often unscrupulous in their collection activities.

Before we talk about what you *possibly* allocate to pay them right now, let's get clear about several things.

First, these people are NOT your friends. I'm sure in "real life" they are probably nice people, but they have been trained to do anything within their legal rights (and many times, beyond their legal rights) in order to try to get payments from you.

Second, there is a long list of items that debt collectors are not allowed to do. I became much stronger in dealing with collection agencies once I learned the rules (knowledge is power!). I posted a pdf document that I found on the Federal Trade Commission website (FTC) that summarizes fair collection practices. (Go to BlastAwayYourDebt.com.)

I'll tell you what I did with my accounts in collections while I was working to get back on track financially. I didn't pay them, I didn't return their endless phone messages, and, if they did happen to catch me on the phone, I made absolutely no commitments whatsoever.

Here's what I would say, "I'm sorry, but today I'm not able to make any kind of commitment regarding this account."

They'd say, "So you're telling me you don't plan to pay this?"

I'd say, "No, that isn't what I said. As I said, today I am not in a position to make any kind of commitment."

They'd say, "Can we set-up a post-dated check for $52.00?"

I'd say, "As I explained, today I am not in a position to make a commitment. Obviously it's important to me that I don't make a promise that I'm not sure I'm able to keep."

They'd say, "To prevent your account from reporting negatively to the credit bureaus, we need to set-up some sort of payment today." (And since my credit score was already in the toilet, so that really didn't motivate me!)

And I'd say, "I have now explained four times that today, I am not in a position to make any kind of commitment to you. Now I realize that you are trained and paid commissions when you get me to do that, but let me ask you this question – what part of my explanation are you NOT understanding?"

Then I'd ask to speak to their supervisor (and most of the time they hung up the phone).

As I explained earlier, at this time, it's better not to talk to them. I'm not saying that you won't eventually pay the bill off. It's a debt that you created and hopefully you want to pay it. You just can't do it today.

I told creditors to stop calling me at work (and if they chose to persist, I would take legal action).

I told them when they threatened to report me to the credit bureaus that my credit score was already trashed, and I certainly

understood if they needed to report a late payment.

And although I never did it, I was fully prepared to send out "cease and desist" letters to collection agencies that after I specifically told them to stop contacting me.

I can reduce this expense by: _____ per month

How are you doing?

Before we review the final category for reducing expenses, how are you doing so far? Have you been totally amazed at the amount of money you have been able to "find" in your bills?

Look at the total amount that you have reduced your monthly payments by right now (and give yourself a gold stamp!).

Have you reached break-even – or even better, *are your monthly bills less than your monthly income?*

Now…keep going. There's only one category left to talk about, but it's a good one.

Other Expenses

It's time to start paying attention. It's so easy to spend money unconsciously (kind of like eating unconsciously) – you leave the house with $40 bucks, and return home empty-handed – and often, you're not sure where the money went.

Let's discuss several places where you might be spending money unnecessarily. I'm going to share the list of expenses that I eliminated, or at least reduced, and I'm going to challenge you to add to it.

a) *Eating out or buying take-out.*

This is an expense you can eliminate immediately. I know – after a long week, the last thing that you feel like doing is cooking on a Friday night, but you are on a mission. You are taking control of your finances to change your life, so you can do this. Think about it – one pizza a week at $15 is $60 per month. Four trips through a fast food joint is probably $35 to $40.

How much would you estimate you spend each month on eating out? Are you willing to eliminate it? (Remember – your financial freedom is at stake here!)

I can reduce this expense by: _____ per month

My true confession: When my finances were in a desperate state, I got "turned on" to ramen noodles. I could buy a six-pack for less than $2 and it was my lunch for a week. (I actually started to like the stuff, too!)

b) *Coffee or other legal stimulants*

Yes, I like my "morning jolt" as much as the next guy. But one medium cup at the local "java joint" was $1.86. A big can of the cheap stuff (yes, I also cut out the expensive brands) cost $8.99 on sale, and lasted about a month.

I can reduce this expense by: _____ per month

c) *Local Health Club*

At one point, I worked with a personal trainer to the tune of about $300 per month (not to mention the travel costs to get to his facility at the crack of dawn).

I can walk down the street at the special discounted rate of "no charge," and I invested in a few weights, along with a Russian Kettleball for less than $50, in order to exercise at home.

I can reduce this expense by: _____ per month

d) *Books*

I love to read, and I love my books. I was spending, on average, $40 per month at the local bookstore. But guess what – they have these things called "libraries" where they'll loan them to you for FREE. You can also borrow books on your Kindle or Kindle app, depending on your membership level.

I can reduce this expense by: _____ per month

e) Entertainment

I love movies. And I love to watch them at the theater, with the big bucket of buttered popcorn and a drink. I decided I needed to keep movies as an expense that I wasn't willing to completely give-up. After all, I had already sacrificed my morning coffee and my weekly pizza.

So here's what I did. I researched all the local theaters to find the best deal. Turned out there was a great theater, very close to where I was living, that has $4 matinees on first run movies. They also have a special deal on the popcorn (the BIG bucket for $4.25).

At most theaters, the cost was at least $20 per movie. I can reduce this expense by: _____ per month

f) hair appointments

I was going to the local up-scale salon to get my hair colored (yikes – did I just admit that?) and cut. The cost was about $125 with tips, every four to five weeks.

I completely eliminated this expense. No, I didn't take on the "Cruela Devil" look, with a big stripe of gray growing out. Instead, I found a brand of "do-it-yourself" dye that costs $6.94 per box.

And, as much as I prefer keeping my hair in a short cut, I let it grow for a while.

When my bangs were driving me crazy (on most days, a short trip), I handed a friend at work my office scissors and asked her to chop my bangs off. Although she was nervous, I assured her that the stuff will grow back. A couple minutes later – I had bangs.

And, I switched shampoo and conditioner. The bottles I was buying at the salon were costing about $45 (they were big bottles, but still - $45??). The cheap stuff from Target is $2.99.

I can reduce this expense by: _____ per month

g) grooming (manicures, pedicures, acrylic nails)

I wasn't spending money on these when my finances took the plunge, but had I been, I'd eliminate the expense. You can do this at home yourself.

I can reduce this expense by: _____ per month

h) sporting events

I know, you're a die hard hockey fan; or you've had season tickets for a pro football team for the last 10 years. Let me remind you that I have been telling you throughout the entire book that this wasn't going to be easy – but it will be worth it. So once again, suck it up.

Let me tell you the "Tim and Mary" story (not their real names). I met this couple when they came to me (when I was in the mortgage business), wanting to refinance their home for the third time in less than 3 years. Yes, they were among part of the crowd that over-spent, then, since their home was appreciating quite rapidly, they refinanced, sucked out the equity, paid off all of their credit cards, and started the process of living high on the hog all over again.

I had to give them the bad news – they had reached the point where they were maxed out. They didn't have any equity to suck out of their house and there was no way we could proceed with a refinance.

They started to make some good financial decisions, but that was short-lived. Here were their choices:

- They put their home on the market, and immediately started looking for a lower-priced property in the same town.
- Found a house priced at $300,000 (Slightly higher than what they originally paid for the home they were now selling!), and decided they had to proceed

with that purchase <u>before</u> selling their other property. The "new" house was 15 years old, and needed several maintenance items done (including a new liner for the pool in the backyard).

- With the help of relatives, they absorbed mortgages on two properties for 4 months until their home sold (because they had refinanced so many times, the mortgage payment on the house they were selling was around $3400 per month). They basically threw away $13,600 on a house they were no longer living in.

- They were fortunate to get an offer on the house they were selling (it was right when the market was starting to turn). They still had to bring about $8,000 to the closing table just to get the transaction done.

- When they moved into the "old house" they bought all new appliances (on a credit card), because they didn't like the "old ones" (which worked just fine).

- Tim changed jobs during this whole process, and didn't have a clue that in doing so, his annual income had dropped by more than $20,000 per year.

You might be wondering why I'm telling you all of this under the category of "sports." Turns out that "Tim and Mary" had two season tickets to the Minnesota Wild games (to the tune of over $1500 per season ticket – i.e. more than $3000.00). Give me a break, the games are televised! This family was headed towards financial ruin, but they held on tightly to those tickets. (They also kept the riding lawn mower for a 60x80 yard, and a long list of other toys, but that's another story.)

I can reduce this expense by: _____ per month

i) other hobbies

Hobbies are great – as long as you don't have to spend a fortune on them right now.

If you spend your weekends doing woodworking, at least for now, you don't need to "invest" in another tool.

My friend is an avid quilter and makes beautiful creations. Each time she goes to a quilt store, she comes home with a stack of fabric (and has enough in the cupboards of her craft room to make quilts for the next 20 years). She told me last week that she won't allow herself to buy anymore fabric until she has completed several quilts.

How much money can you free up, for now, by cutting back on a hobby? Or, is there a way for you to turn a hobby into a small business, so it can make money and give you some great tax write-offs? (More about that later.)

I can reduce this expense by: _____ per month

j) magazine and newspaper subscriptions

I'm all for reading magazines, following an industry in trade magazines, or keeping up on the daily news. But those rags are probably costing you anywhere from $80 to $250 per year, depending on how many you subscribe to, and what the fee is for the subscription.

So many publications are available online that you can probably access the majority of those publications through the internet (and what the heck, you'll save a few trees).

I eliminated my newspaper ($52 every four months), and two magazine subscriptions ($18 and $30 per year)

I can reduce this expense by: _____ per month

k) groceries

I'm not in any way suggesting that you don't purchase groceries (in fact, groceries are a better option than eating take-out or fast food), but what are you buying while you're there?

My tips to minimize your grocery bill are:

1) never go to the grocery store without a list

2) clip and use coupons (but only for things that you were going to purchase anyway).

3) go into the store with a limited amount of money (or pre-purchased gift card, using my gift-card technique), and keep a running estimate of your total due <u>as you shop.</u> It makes it a lot easier to pass by some of the junk food, or the expensive bag of cookies, when you're cognizant of what you're spending.

4) Buy some things in bulk. Even though I'm single, I bought large

packages of chicken, hamburger, salmon and pork chops (sorry vegetarians!), split them into small quantity packages, and kept them in my freezer. I had about 3 months' worth on hand, so I had to shop less frequently (and fewer trips to the grocery store meant savings!).

5) Be careful with items that are perishable. I realized I was constantly throwing out half-full bags of lettuce and strawberries that never got washed. I stopped buying those

items. I figured I'd rather do without than waste the money on spoilage.

I can reduce this expense by: _____ per month

l) CDs, music downloads, video rentals

Believe it or not, you will survive without adding the latest tune to your iPod. And, if you're a movie freak like I am, you are probably getting rental DVDs in the mail.

I'm sure your iPod is already loaded with great tunes. And why not find a friend with a movie membership and share the DVDs, while splitting the cost?

I can reduce this expense by: _____ per month

m) pets

I know I'm going to "ruffle some feathers" with this one. But please, hear me out, and give this some careful consideration.

First, I have to tell you that I am a pet lover. Right now I have two cats and a dog, and over the years I've had a small herd of horses, several other cats, and a couple different dogs. I love animals (the furry kind, not the "men acting poorly" kind). So when I ask you to determine if there are ways you can reduce the costs of your pets, believe me - it's tough.

My belief is that if you are going to have the animals, then you need to make a strong commitment to take good care of them. That being said, are there ways you can cut some costs?

Do you take the dog to a groomer each month? Perhaps you can do it yourself at home? Or, are you buying Fluffy the most expensive food recommended by your veterinarian? Consider asking the vet if there is a cheaper alternative.

And, if you are in dire straits, then you may need to make the tough choice to find your pet another home – temporarily or permanently. I know, that would kill me, and it would be a last resort, but think of your pet's well-being first. (Again, I'm the woman who had a $2,000 vet bill because my cat spent a weekend in a "luxury suite" at the local university's vet school because she couldn't keep her food down, so it is really tough for me to say you may need to give up a pet. But if you are at the point that you need to choose between feeding your kids versus feeding your pets – obviously your kids come first!)

I switched my cats to a less-expensive food, and started buying cat litter in bulk at Sam's Club.

I can reduce this expense by: _____ per month

n) *other expenses*

Now we need to talk about that elusive category that I didn't think of: other. What else are you spending money on? Can you reduce any additional costs?

Make a list of any additional expense that you have; and figure out ways to reduce, or better yet, eliminate that expense.

I can reduce this expense by: _____ per month

Whew – you made it!

First, congratulations. You made it through that very tough, but empowering, exercise. I'm guessing you were surprised at how much money you've been letting slip through the cracks. At this stage, I'm hoping that you are well beyond *"break even"* and you're feeling on top of the world.

Give yourself some of those imaginary gold stamps that I explained because you have made great progress towards financial freedom!

Now, take a quick break (meaning, use the restroom), refill your beverage, and keep going. You've made such great progress; there is no reason to stop now.

Don't hate me, but….

No rest for people striving to achieve financial freedom, because here's what you need to do next: **Go through the list again!**

If you're not at break even, look for some additional expenses to reduce or eliminate. And if you are past break even (meaning you have money left after all the bills are paid), I'm still challenging you to free up some additional dollars.

I know, you just *painfully* sifted through every expense that you have, and made sacrifice after sacrifice to decrease your monthly bills. You're already feeling like the toddler who just had their favorite blanket ripped away for its monthly laundering. But hopefully, you're also seeing a bigger and brighter picture for your future. Hopefully you're seeing a little flicker of financial light at the end of a deep and dark cave. You started to take control, and you did a great job.

What I'm going to ask you to do now separates the people who are incredibly motivated to take control of their finances, from those who, deep down, are hoping a distant relative who has no heirs gets run over by a Mack truck.

(Get it? They're still waiting for somebody else to provide the solution to their financial problems.)

The next step, to work towards break even (and if you have already reached break even, keep going anyway) is to squeeze even more money out.

So right now, go down your list of monthly expenses one more time and ask yourself,

"Is there anything else that I can reduce or eliminate or change in this category that will help me cut this expense?"

Keep asking yourself, "Is this really something I *need*, or just something that I *want*?" Challenge yourself, make it a game, have fun finding more money that you can free up in your finances. Remember, this will impact the rest of your life.

When you're finished - add up the total amount of expenses that you have eliminated or reduced. Amazing, isn't it? You can "find" all kind of money when you work at it.

Money that is Slipping through the Cracks

If you haven't been paying attention, it's possible that you don't have a clue where your money is going. If not, then let me issue this challenge.

For *at least one month*, (and once you do this - you'll find it actually becomes fun and addicting - and you'll make it a long-term habit) I challenge you to track every cent that you spend. Get a very small notebook, or even fold up some paper that you can tuck into your pocket, and every time you spend even one little penny, write it down.

You might be really surprised about where your money is going.

When I did this, I realized that I was clueless about the amount I was spending on fast food and junk food. (I told you I'm a mood eater!)

My total was about $200 per month – from pizzas to swinging through a burger joint to ice cream. Since I was paying cash, I "guessed" it was $50 or $60. Wrong! I was spending about $200. Ouch.

Before we move on to the next important step – *Earn More* – let's do a quick review. You've already made major progress (give yourself more gold stamps!):

- You made a commitment that you will not go further into debt today (and you will make that same commitment to yourself every single day).

- You have started saving money for extreme emergencies only – even if it is $5 bucks a week (hopefully more!).

- You opened your mail, sorted it into its appropriate categories, designated a specific location in the house (in a box or drawer) where you will keep the bills, you made a commitment to open your mail and review your bills at a regular, scheduled time each week.

- You made a list of your monthly bills, along with the details of each bill.

- You added regular monthly expenses to that list.

- And, you added expenses that don't occur monthly, such as licenses, etc., and prorated them to a monthly expense.

- You determined if you are earning enough to cover your "basic needs" of food, clothing, medicine and shelter.

- You prioritized the remainder of your bills by numbering them 1-13, and listed your credit cards in order, based on lowest to highest minimum payment. You determined which you are able to pay now – and which have to wait, temporarily.

- To work towards "break even," you reviewed every one of your monthly expenses, figured out ways to reduce or eliminate them, and took all necessary action (meaning called companies to discontinue services, etc.).

- And, after you eliminated your monthly expenses, you scrutinized the list again, and found even more ways to reduce your monthly costs.

- If you didn't know where your money was going, you've started to track it.

CONGRATULATIONS!!! Keep going!! The next section will be fun!

Step Nine: Earn More / Increase Income

Now let's talk about the other part of our equation — *income*. Remember:

Money left at the end of the month = income – expenses

There are lots of ways to add to your income, so I encourage you to start thinking creatively. These ideas are intended to get you started.

1) Hidden Money Around the House

First, let's review some ideas for ways to generate extra cash — not necessarily income, but some extra cash.

Let's say that you have a couple "nagging bills" that you'd really like to eliminate.

For example, let's say you have an old medical bill with a balance of about $300.00. You're tired of it and you want to pay it off once and for all.

Look around the house and figure out what you can sell to generate some extra cash. These days you can sell things through ebay or Craig's list with minimal or no charge. Or, have a garage sale!

Start the list. What can you sell on Craig's list, ebay, or through a garage sale right now so you can add some cash to your savings and pay off a couple bills right now?

Obviously you need to be cautious when you use any of these services. Here's what I sold: a video camera, appliances, books and audio programs, a couple Lladro statues, a treadmill that was sitting in my basement, some old silver certificates, books and audio tape programs, and Longaberger baskets.

I always think of the saying, "Your trash might be other people's treasures" when I look around the house for things of value.

And think about all the people on "Antique Road Show" who are surprised when some old piece of artwork that was tucked in their attic for the last 50 years, turns out to be worth several thousand dollars.

If you need some ideas for things people are selling, look around on ebay. List your items, sell them, and manage the money within your plan. (Save a portion – at least 10% - and use the rest to pay off that nagging bill!)

2) *Make More in Your Current Job:*

Next, how can you increase your income at work? Can you work overtime? Can you apply for a promotion? Can you ask for a raise? Can you attend some company-paid training to add to your skills?

I think it's important to get very clear about your talents and skills. Right now, make a list of your skills, training, and areas of expertise (this can be a great foundation for an updated resume, too). This is not a time to be shy or modest. Also list the additional training or certification you would like to acquire to help you get a promotion.

Talk to your supervisor and express your desire to earn more, both by working additional hours and by advancing within the company. Ask what is required to make that happen. Ask your supervisor to be your career mentor; then start proving your worth by working above and beyond what is expected of you.

Express your desire to attend any training that the company is offering. For example, although I wasn't in a "sales job," I asked the lead trainer if I could attend any classes that were being conducted for the sales staff. It's a great way to prepare for the next position, and show your passion for the future position.

And, keep your "list of successes" so you can review these with your supervisor regularly.

Watch all company job postings. When you apply for an internal promotion, keep your "list of successes" available for your interview.

To get a promotion, it means it's time to become a "model employee" and to become a "self-promoter" so you get noticed for your outstanding performance. If you've been messing up in the past – either with your attitude or your performance, let your supervisor know that you were wrong, and that from this day forward

your performance will be well beyond expectations. Then do it!

Also, check on classes being offered as part of the stimulus package through local colleges and community colleges. This can be a great way to acquire additional knowledge and skills for job advancement.

3) Add an Income Stream

You've probably considered it already. A third way to generate more money is by adding another income stream – either with a part-time job or a part-time business.

First, let's talk about a part-time job. Can you find a position that might lead to a great full-time job? Things to think about:

- the schedule
- where this new opportunity might take you
- the company (review its industry, and any potential public information such as stock prices, historical information, press releases, news articles, etc.)
- How will you having a part-time job affect you family?

Consider starting a Home Party or Network Marketing Business!

I have to tell you my bias here. There are so many things I love about home party and network marketing businesses. I believe this can be the perfect additional income stream for anyone who is motivated.

Here's why:

1) You have control over your time. You can work as much, or as little, as you choose.

2) You have control over your schedule. You can work around child care issues, schedule as many hours as you choose, and take time off for vacations without asking for permission.

3) You can get going quickly. Literally, depending on the company, you can sign-up today, and start selling…today!

4) Most companies have very minimal start-up or starter kit costs (anywhere from $20 to $997). There aren't many businesses you can start for such a low cost.

5) There is absolute minimal risk. You aren't taking out business loans, or maxing out credit cards. Worst case scenario is you choose not to continue and give your samples to your relatives for holiday gifts.

6) You can take advantage of the entire compensation plan by sponsoring others into the business. That's a great way to get additional revenue by helping others succeed.

7) There can be tax advantages when you can write off some small business and home office expenses (check with your tax professional).

8) This might even become an incredibly lucrative business venture for you (I built my business to annual commissions that ranged from $105,000 to $135,000 for 11 years straight. Although I'm not guaranteeing anything about the amount you can earn - since there are lots of different factors - I want you to know the potential.)

A Financial Success Story - thanks to a home party business.

Helene Leonard describes her family's financial mess as "a catastrophic nightmare."

She works full-time as a school teacher and has a part-time home-party business with Thirty-One Gifts; her husband, Joe, is a police officer; and they have two young children — Natalie and Christian.

Here's Helene's financial success story:

We were going through life, doing pretty well, making decent money, and living as though there was no end to the money we were making. We just didn't pay attention to where our money was going - and we made some pretty poor choices.

But that's when life took an interesting twist.

My husband, along with other senior level Police Officers in his city, were required to take demotions due to city budgeting issues. This helped the city avoid layoffs for many other police officers. But with that demotion came a huge cut in salary for Joe, and our family.

Overnight, we went from "not paying attention to anything" to being faced with the reality that we could possibly lose our home, if we didn't make some immediate changes.

As we looked closely at our finances, and figured out where we were at, after paying just minimum payments on all our bills, and childcare expenses - we had a measly $65 left per week for our family of four to live on.

I was scared to death.

We were making a combined income of six figures. But we were living beyond our means and not paying attention.

We had taken out pension loans, we had credit card debt, we had a second mortgage on our home. We had 11 different debts that had to be paid every month.

Our total consumer debt was about $220,000.

At the same time - we both had extremely high credit scores. We thought because our credit scores were so high that we must be doing something right.

But as we started to really dig into our financial mess - we learned that wasn't really accurate.

It was terrifying. We were scared. We were angry. We couldn't believe we made decisions that got us into this situation. It took a toll on our marriage. We didn't fight. We didn't argue. We didn't blame. But we both felt so guilty that we became withdrawn from each other.

I was in panic mode, so I went searching for information. I came across some of Dave Ramsey's books. I read his first book and it changed my life — changed our lives.

We, as a family, decided we had to get it together. We created a written budget, and started implementing our plan to pay down our debts. Joe worked overtime as much as possible. I tutored math students. We did anything and everything we could to make extra money.

Following Dave Ramsey's plan, our first step was to save $1000. In the past, the only time we had money in savings was when we got a tax refund or some other unexpected payment. We never left it in savings for very long. It wasn't "intentional."

This was the first time we actually worked to put money away. We scraped together that $1000 as fast as we could. That's when we realized "we can do this!"

We started working Dave's "snowball" plan - where we lined up our bills from smallest to largest, and put every extra penny towards paying off the smallest bill first.

When we paid off our first credit card - we got a little glimmer of hope.

We worked together, looked at our bills each month, and we wrote down exactly how we would spend every penny we earned.

We started telling our money what it was going to do. It felt great.

Around that time, my best friend, Dondrea, joined Thirty-One Gifts (as she jokes, to pay for her Target shopping addiction). She was hosting a "launch party" to kick off her business, and I didn't go. I was too embarrassed to be there because I wasn't going to be able to buy anything.

A few days later, Dondrea asked me if selling Thirty-One was something I wanted to do, too. I had no sales experience, and I never attended a home party in my life - not ever.

So I ended up going to one of her parties to observe. I thought, "Maybe this is something I can do," and made the decision to join Dondrea's team for a minimal $99 investment.

At first, my biggest goal was to earn enough to pay for the bags that I loved!

But my business quickly helped us attack our debt even faster.

I started taking my entire Thirty-One commissions and applying the entire amount to whichever creditor was at the top of the list to pay off. That way the money was never missed.

Working together, Joe and I have paid off everything, except for one student loan, in just 3 1/2 years. We were also able to make home renovations using cash.

This past summer we went on a family vacation that was entirely paid for - in advance - with the commissions from my Thirty-One business.

When you're in the place of darkness, and you're scared, living from paycheck-to-paycheck - you stop dreaming. You're just trying to survive. We never want to have that feeling again - and neither should you!

These days Helene is dreaming big! She is building her Thirty-One business very quickly - because she is passionate about helping people take control of their finances - the way she and Joe did.

(For more information - go to: Helene-Leonard.com.)

Before Signing-up with a Home Party or Network Marketing Company - Do Your Homework!

The cost of the starter kit is good information. But there are many more factors I recommend you consider when choosing the right company for you.

I've prepared a special report for you called **"What to Consider When Choosing a Home Party or Network Marketing Company."**

Go to: **BlastAwayYourDebt.com** to download your copy.

On the following pages you'll find listings for several different independent consultants. They are all highly successful in their businesses, and I strongly recommend you look through their websites and reach out to learn more.

Meredith Yost, Albuquerque, NM
408 221-2840   www.wine4u247.com
mywineshop247@gmail.com

Are you a wine lover?

WineShop at Home (WSAH) offers limited edition hand-crafted wines, gift baskets, gift wines, and custom labeled wines (perfect for advertising, or as special gifts for your best clients). But here's what is truly unique. Our collection is strictly available through Wine Consultants - either at private in-home wine tastings, or through each consultant's personalized company website.

Whether you consider yourself to be a "wine expert," or the extent of your knowledge is strictly "it's white" or "it's red," WineShop at Home will give you all the training and information you need to easily help your hostesses and customers choose their favorite wines.

WSAH makes being in business simple and fun. That includes:

- an excellent compensation plan
- fabulous replicated websites - giving each wine consultant a strong web presence
- back office updates to Facebook
- twitter and other social media applications
- a monthly newsletter to share with your customers
- extensive training and support - both from the home office, and your upline
- all-expense paid rewards trips
- an annual convention - held right in the heart of the California wine country

Please go to my website and see for yourself what we have for products and specials. What are you waiting for? Give me a call to discuss how you can have your own wine business or if you just want to get started right away, you can go to my website and JOIN online.

Enjoy tea *and* make money?
Yes, with Great Big Teas you can do both!

You can introduce whole-leaf teas and quality accessories to groups of friends or separately to individuals and earn Personal Sales Commission and Personal Sales Bonuses.

Earn even more if you'd like. When you choose to become a leader by introducing and sharing the Great Big Teas opportunity with other people, you will be paid on the bonus volume of others.

Part-time or full-time, you can be successful as a Great Big Teas consultant. It's your business. You get to decide how big it will be. The greater your efforts, the greater your rewards!

How did Lisa Davidsohn, Founder & CEO and Renee Gluck, Co-Founder & CAO come up with the concept? Lisa has always enjoyed tea. She started drinking supermarket tea at the age of four. In her twenties, Lisa tasted her first cup of whole-leaf tea and was immediately smitten. Over the years, Lisa developed her palate and effectively sought out the higher-quality whole-leaf teas.

Lisa introduced her friend, Renee Gluck, to the world of whole-leaf teas. Renee, a coffee drinker, has gained, over the years, quite an appreciation for whole-leaf tea. Together, they attend tea-based trade shows, in search of high-quality, distinctive teas to be enjoyed by themselves, their families, friends and customers.

Share their passion for tea? Call Lisa or Renee at 877-734-8488 and ask about their income opportunity. You can email them at: info@greatbigteas.com.

Website: *https://www.greatbigteas.com/1*

Facebook: *https://www.facebook.com/greatbigteas*

I'm Beth Millman, an Independent petPro with pawTree, a company that specializes in customized pet nutrition as well as supplements and treats for your furry friend.

Every day I get to work my passion for pets with my dog Quincy, while helping other pet parents find the best nutrition and supplements for their pets. pawTree also has exclusive beds, blankets, collars and bowls that cannot be found in retail for spoiling your pup. Plus, our 3NFree program allows people to get their dog's food for free, and as a Paw Club member, receive great specials and discounts on shipping for all EZ ship orders.

pawTree's food is made in the USA, and has no corn, wheat, soy, artificial colors, flavors or preservatives, and real meat is always the first ingredient. I was a customer before joining pawTree as an independent petPro because my dog Quincy fell in love with the products. Seeing his reaction, and learning about the "pawsibilities" of developing my own business and additional income stream that can be done part-time around your present job or full-time, made me say Two Paws Up!

Curious? If so, drop me a line at quincycology@gmail.com or at 213-986-7918, and I promise to send you a free pawTree treat sample, along with more information about pawTree's business opportunity and customized pet nutrition, including how you can qualify for our 3NFree program and Paw Club membership. I look forward to connecting with you.
www.pawtree.com/quincycology

Thirty-One's products will put you in the spotlight every time you're out and about!

- Unique, Personalized Bags
- Storage Products/Totes
- Personalized Gifts
- Wallets/Accessories
- NEW! Gorgeous high-end faux leather line!

Enjoy new specials each month on my Thirty-One website: http://www.SoManyCuteBags.com.

FREE GIFT when you subscribe to my newsletter: http://bit.ly/31specials

Want free and discounted products? Contact me (31leader@gmail.com) about these options:
- Home, Office, Catalog Parties
- Online/Facebook Parties
- Bridal/Baby Showers, etc.
- Fundraisers (I offer 30% to your organization!)

Our income opportunity is incredible. You can be flexible so you won't sacrifice precious family time. Join for only $99; receive a beautiful kit to start off strong; earn 25% commission beginning with your very first sale; opportunity to earn more when YOU are ready.

Some perks I've earned: 6 free all-expenses paid trips to the Riviera Maya, Cancun and the Dominican Republic; over $4,000 in Gift Cards, Tiffany Jewelry, and over $10,000 in Cash Bonuses.

Thanks to Thirty-One, I am now debt-free! I want YOU to have it all, too, because YOU deserve it!

No experience necessary. Free training is provided. Isn't it time you love the life you live?
- Request a catalog and/or more information at http://bit.ly/31specials
- Receive a FREE GIFT when you subscribe to my monthly specials newsletter
- Shop my store 24/7: http://www.SoManyCuteBags.com

Phyllis O'Neill, Thirty-One Independent Senior Executive Director
31leader@gmail.com * www.SoManyCuteBags.com

Get Started and Build Success

Getting started with Paparazzi is easy and can be a life changing experience. Most of Paparazzi's Consultants not only use Paparazzi as a way to generate additional income for their families, but also as a way to have fun, enjoy their friends and family, and share something with their acquaintances that can build lasting relationships. Above all, what Paparazzi Consultants love is that it's easy!

Sell fashion jewelry for $5.00 a piece and make 45% profit!

Sell online or get a kit to use for parties or craft shows.

Help your customers feed their $5 habit!

It is as simple as visiting **paparazziaccessories.com/13591** to choose a starter kit and signup.

Contact Chris Clark, independent consultant, at
paparazzichris@gmail.com

facebook.com/PaparazziByChris

beautiful inside & out

RUBY ℞ RIBBON
INDEPENDENT STYLIST

I'm **Marie Street**, an Independent Stylist and Leader with **Ruby Ribbon**, a company dedicated to helping ALL women look and feel beautiful inside and out.

As a wife and mother, I love helping to empower others. It's so much fun to style women in our clothing as well as an honor to mentor other Stylists and watch them achieve their own dreams and goals.

Ruby Ribbon has been called the "BEST" Shapewear on the market. I fell in love with Ruby Ribbon's products because of their versatility. Not only do all of our pieces mix and match well with each other they'll also enhance pieces you love that are already in your own closet. Our three categories of clothing – Shaping Essentials, where our mark is truly unique, Shapewear, and Fashion Layers have something for everyone.

Do you love fashion?
If so, contact me at *ditchurbra@gmail.com* **or 678-856-3876** to find out more about this ground floor, rapidly growing business opportunity – perfect for anyone who wants to build a six figure income leveraging the $10 billion dollar a year Shapewear Industry.

Carole O. Bloch is an Outfitter Leader with Initial Outfitters, a company founded in 2006 and based in Auburn, Alabama. Initial Outfitters offers personalized jewelry and boutique type shopping!

Initial Outfitters' home parties allow women to enjoy time with friends while updating their wardrobes or shopping for gifts. A catalog with over 96 pages of products provides guests with one-of-a-kind jewelry and gifts for all occasions.

Carole began her direct sales career as a source of extra income for her family over 23 years ago. During this time, she has met many women who have become dear friends and has helped a large number of those women begin their own direct sales businesses. Helping other women realize their potential and find their niche is what drives Carole in her business. She has watched many women find gifts and abilities they did not know they possessed and has been able to witness many shining moments in their lives!!

Carole's Initial Outfitters career began just over two years ago and she believes she has found the place she will stay. Her love for Initial Outfitters grows more each day as she becomes better acquainted with the owners and management team of her company. Carole attributes her success with Initial Outfitters to unique products, a very generous hostess program, superior home office customer service, and excellent training systems. An Initial Outfitters career is fun, easy and very rewarding!!!

To find out more about building your own Initial Outfitters business and/or see our unique product line, **email Carole at *caroleaha22@aol.com* and type IO Info in the subject line.** If you would like your own copy of our beautiful catalog, include your name and mailing address.

dōTERRA®

Wellness Advocate

I'm very excited to have the opportunity to share my good fortune with you.

My name is **Julie Inman and I'm an Independent Wellness Advocate with doTERRA Essential Oils**. When I was introduced to doTERRA, I had no idea how my life was going to change, physically and financially.

A friend invited me to learn about the benefits of essential oils, and by the end of the class I knew this was for me. What I learned, was that we have an alternative in managing our health and wellness.

doTERRA offers many options for healthy living. Here are a few examples...
- Certified Pure Therapeutic Grade Essential Oils (CPTG)
- Whole Food Supplements
- Weight Management
- Respiratory Function
- Skin Irritation
- Digestive Support
- Hormonal and Emotional Balance
- Personal Care, Cleaning Products...and many more.

If you would like to learn more about Essential Oils please visit my website, call or email:
www.fullytransformedjulie.com,
fullytransformedjulie@gmail.com
828-279-1871

Rosalie Duong is a **Managing Director with MICHE** — a company that distributes those amazing versatile handbags that you can change — in an instant.

MICHE®

fashion at the speed of life™

Tired of switching from handbag to handbag, depending on the occasion or outfit? Women love MICHE bags because, instead of moving all of your important personal items from one purse to the next, MICHE's ingenious design allows you to simply change the covers to go from a casual luncheon to a formal dinner party.

Rosalie joined MICHE because she loves the products, it's incredibly easy to book parties, and it's a business she can work around her busy family life. She wants to inspire and help other women build a part-time business, or a full-time career.

Rosalie credits her success to her networking skills and is passionate that networking is a skill every home party or network marketing consultant needs to learn, and can easily learn, with her coaching. She has created a special report called "Network Your Way to Success," and would love to share it with you.

Simply go to **https://rosalieduong.leadpages.net/network-your-way-to-success/** to immediately download the report. Rosalie will also include some information about this ground-floor & fast-growing business opportunity — perfect for anyone who wants to build a six-figure income leveraging the $9 billion US handbag market.

Helene Leonard - Ind. Director with Thirty-one Gifts

I hope you read my financial success story that was featured earlier in this book.

My husband and I were at the stage where we had taken control of how we spent every single dime we earned - and we were making progress.

But joining Thirty-one Gifts helped us dig out of our financial mess - **years ahead of schedule.**

At the same time, I found a business that I'm truly passionate about, and have so much fun when I'm out holding parties, or helping my team members get their businesses started.

Thirty-one offers an amazing collection of trendy, affordable products that help organize your life.

For example, our zip-top organizing tote is perfect for busy Moms (it even has seven pockets - so you can keep everything right at your fingertips); our "Cindy Tote" is a favorite among professional women with its classic design and roomy interior - you can easily fit your laptop and other work essentials.

We carry purses, thermals, totes, wallets, utility bags, accessory bags - and much more.

I started this business with absolutely no sales experience. These products are easy to sell because women love them.

To learn more about my financial journey - and additional information about the Thirty-one products and business - please go to my website:

helene-leonard.com; or email me: helene@helene-leonard.com

Meet Nancy Ellington:

I'm an entrepreneur with a phenomenal company called **Ardyss International**. It has been in business for over 20 years.

The best way to describe Ardyss is by saying "our products makeover peoples' lives - first on the outside, then from the inside," an amazing 2 step system.

We start with our amazing "Body Magic" garment. Put on this therapeutic medical grade undergarment, and you will immediately drop two-to-three dress or belt sizes. No diets, no exercise, no pills, no surgery. This undergarment has been specially designed to reshape your figure in all the right places and gives the body a treatment each time it is worn.

People feel amazing wearing it. They look and feel more confident instantly. That's how we give them a makeover on the outside.

Next, we go to work to continue their makeover - but now, from the inside out.

Our cellular nutritional products help people who are looking for pain relief, struggle with low or no energy, insomnia, weight management, and much more. I'm not making any medical claims. Our products provide antioxidants, and help balance your body's pH levels. Ugly diseases simply can't live in an alkaline environment. I've heard many testimonials during our consultant calls about Ardyss' products helps them manage their high blood pressure, high cholesterol, diabetes, and more.

We also have wraps (great to detox, tone and firm your body), and an anti-aging skin care collection that leaves your face feeling smooth and soft.

Finally, the Ardyss business opportunity helps people makeover their financial lives. Whether you're interested in making some part time cash, or "quit-your-day-job" income - the possibilities are endless with our company.

I would love to share more and most of all give you a **free personal questionnaire** to help assess your overall health. As **a bonus I'd like to send you a sample of our healthy coffee as my gift to you.** Fill out your information by going to **http://goo.gl/zfwbi3** now or liveahealthylife2@gmail.com

Nancy Ellington 863-370-6243 call/text
Website: www.ardyss.net/msnell

Manage Your Business Finances Well

If you currently have bad financial habits, chances are strong that you will also carry those bad habits right into your business. The result: you'll dig yourself into an even deeper hole.

Here's some tips to consider about managing your business finances:

1) Open a separate checking and savings account that you strictly use for your business. That will make it easier to track and monitor your financials.

2) Be careful that you don't spend unnecessary money up-front. Initially you don't NEED every sample; business cards can wait; you don't have to buy special displays; and you can dig up a suitcase to carry your samples, rather than buying your company's logo bag. Sure - all of these things are helpful - but they aren't NECESSARY to successfully launch your business.

3) Pay yourself - just like a job. Whether you do this once a month, twice a month, or weekly (I like to do it monthly) - record your income, subtract your business

expenses, save a portion of your profits for business expenses, taxes, etc. (30-40%), and pay yourself the balance.

4) Don't bankrupt your business. Too often consultants will take all their profits from their business account the second it arrives. You want to build up some reserves in your business account for new samples, attending your national conferences, training, etc. You can't do that with confidence if you keep your business broke.

5) Save receipts! One of the many advantages of starting your own business is the tax write-offs. Keep good receipts and records for everything. You can always choose not to write something off - but that is difficult without good records.

(For a special report about managing your business finances easily and effectively, go to: **BlastAwayYourDebt.com**.)

What Happens After You Reach Break Even? – This is Your Tipping Point!

You have made major progress. Doesn't it feel great?

Let's review where you're at so far:

- You made a commitment that you will not go further into debt today (and you will make that same commitment to yourself every single day).

- You have started saving money for extreme emergencies only – even if it is $5 bucks a week (hopefully more!).

- You opened your mail, sorted it into its appropriate categories, designated a specific location in the house (in a box or drawer) where you will keep the bills, you made a commitment to open your mail and review your bills at a regular, scheduled time each week.

- You made a list of your monthly bills, along with the details of each bill.

- You added regular monthly expenses to that list.

- And, you added expenses that don't occur monthly, such as licenses, etc., and prorated them to a monthly expense.

- You determined if you are earning enough to cover your "basic needs" of food, clothing, medicine and shelter.

- You prioritized the remainder of your bills by numbering them 1-11, and listed your credit cards in order, based on lowest to highest minimum payment. You determined which you are able to pay now — and which have to wait, temporarily.

- To work towards "break even," you reviewed every one of your monthly expenses, figured out ways to reduce or eliminate them, and took all necessary action (meaning called companies to discontinue services, etc.).

- And, after you eliminated your monthly expenses, you scrutinized the list again, and found even more ways to reduce your monthly costs.

- If you didn't know where your money was going, you started tracking your expenses.

- You figured out how to generate some extra cash to pay off some nagging bills – by selling items on ebay, Craig's List, or through a garage sale.
- You've looked at ways to increase your monthly income – especially with the option of a starting a home party or network marketing business.

Well done!! You are incredible!! So what's next...??

Increase Your Savings First

Now that you have cruised past break even and you are earning more than your expenses, the very first area we want to address is to start saving more money each month.

Remember when I talked about Maslow's hierarchy of needs? We first focused on your physiological needs of food, clothing and shelter.

By saving money, you will be moving up the ranks to "safety and security," and it is critically important at this step in the process.

Does your employer offer a 401K account? If the answer is yes, and you haven't been investing in it, start immediately -- especially if your employer matches a portion of your deposits (that is like giving yourself an immediate raise).

If, for example, your employer matches 50-percent of your 401K deposit, to 3-percent of your income, then you need to start depositing 6% of your paycheck before taxes into the 401K so you don't leave any of your employer's dollars sitting on the table (your human resources department can assist you with the paperwork).

I believe we need to save at least 10% of our gross earnings, based on principles I learned in many books. ("The Richest Man in Babylon,") for example.)

If you're not ready to save 10-percent yet – that's OK – but start increasing your savings immediately, provided you can stay above **break even.**

I like to start with the 401K deposit because it will come out of your check automatically by your employer. When I started my job, I implemented the 401K payments immediately, and was pleasantly surprised when I pulled up the account six months later and it was worth over $2,000.

In addition to a 401K deposit, you also need to focus on a "liquid" account – for <u>emergencies only</u>.

The savings goal is to have enough in an accessible account to cover at least six months of your expenses, in the unlikely event that you lose your job.

In addition, I recommend putting 10-percent in a wealth building account and 10-percent in another savings account that we'll call a *"giving account,"* for reasons much too complicated to explain here.

After you've increased your monthly savings deposits, it's time to go after debt – aggressively.

Next, we'll start working on paying down debt. Now that you are earning enough money to cover your monthly bills, and you've increased your savings, it's time to go after your debts. We want to start eliminating those bills that have been hanging over your head – one by one.

I like to think of it as though I'm at the shooting range (although I've never actually shot a gun – I've just watched a lot of cop shows), and each bill is posted on a target. The first bill takes some practice, and some focused effort to shoot down. But with each bill I pummel away at, it becomes easier and easier.

From this point forward, every debt you pay off makes a dramatic difference in your financial life. As you continue to "free up" more and more money, and as you continue to increase your income with your home party or network marketing business – you'll be able to save more, invest more, and start to focus on building wealth.

The Smart Way to Pay Off Your Debts – Faster Than You Think You Can!

Next, as you continue down the road to financial freedom, we need to discuss the best strategy to pay off those pesky bills. Obviously some of your bills are expenses that you will never eliminate (food, clothing, shelter, medical expenses, etc.). Yes, you can work to pay off your mortgage, but you will still have property taxes, insurance, possibly homeowner association dues, and utilities. If it applies to you, child care and child support are payments that are more long-term. And the amount and time frame for spousal maintenance (i.e. alimony) can vary, depending on your dissolution agreement.

So let's talk about a strategy to eliminate – forever -- those other bills on the list – namely credit cards, car loans, students loans, loans from relatives or friends, medical bills, past due taxes and collection accounts.

Because you worked so hard to get to break-even, you know, with confidence, that you can make the minimum payments each month on all of your bills. But won't it feel awesome to eliminate these payments altogether?

I can't take credit for this idea – but it works incredibly well – so here goes:

Sort your bill list in order from lowest balance to highest balance (hopefully it already is sorted, with the exception of a credit card or two that have high monthly payments, relative to their balances).

Now – what will it take for you to pay off the bill with the lowest <u>balance?</u> Maybe $200, or just $150, or even less? Whatever the amount - that's the bill you attack with every extra penny you have available - first!

If you make $125 doing one of your home parties this week - you'll take a portion of those profits (strictly a portion because you need to leave some "working capital" in your business account) - and pay all of it towards that bill with the lowest balance.

Attack it with a vengeance. Use this as your first profit goal for your business. You'll be amazed how quickly you can pay off the bill with the lowest balance when you are focused and passionate.

Once this bill is paid off, (**this is the key, so pay close attention here**) you're going to <u>roll the amount of this payment to the next bill on the list.</u>

Here's an example of how this works:

Let's say your credit card bills are as follows:

Credit Card A – Balance $400 – Minimum payment - $25.00

Credit Card B – Balance $600 – Minimum payment - $30.00

Credit Card C – Balance $1000 – Minimum payment - $50.00

Credit Card D – Balance $2000 – Minimum payment - $100.00

You've been following the Financial Freedom Plan, and you have increased your income by $100 per month after taxes (NOTE: This is an extremely conservative figure - especially once you see the potential income you can make with a home party or network marketing business). I'm assuming $20 of the $100 is going to savings, the rest you can apply to your bills.

You will apply ALL of this additional income to Credit Card A, so you are able to make a payment on Credit Card A of $25 + $80 (additional income) – or $105.00 per month.

(Special note: as I mentioned previously - if you are one of my students - I will be challenging you to choose that payment with the lowest balance, and generate enough income in one or two months - to pay it off completely! It's a total blast, and feels amazing when you do this! It's totally possible with a home party or network marketing business!)

You'll continue to make the minimum payment on the other three cards.

Considering interest charges, etc., by paying $105 per month for 4 months, your credit card balances will now be something like this:

Credit Card A – **PAID IN FULL!**

Credit Card B – about $500

Credit Card C – about $880

Credit Card D – about $1700

And now, here's the part that becomes powerful. Once Credit Card A is PAID IN FULL, roll the minimum payment forward to Credit Card B!

You were paying $30 per month on Credit Card B. With the additional payment from Credit Card A ($105.00) – you are now paying $135.00 per month on Credit Card B – and it will be PAID IN FULL in about 4 more months. Time for another happy dance.

Then, take that $135, and add it to what you are paying on Credit Card C. (You were paying $50 per month on Credit Card C – now you'll pay $185 per month.) It will be paid off in another 3-4 months, and you'll roll that payment forward again. Isn't that slick?

Now, with the extra cash you have available – you can deal with collection accounts.

You've got your finances under control, and you now you have money left at the end of the month. So it's time to deal with my "favorite" category (being totally facetious here) – collection accounts.

I believe you should start by contacting the original creditor. They may be prepared to work with you, or they may tell you to contact the collection agency.

Here's my list of suggestions for dealing with these accounts:

1) Ask to speak with a supervisor – always.

2) Everything is negotiable. Think about it – at this stage the creditor didn't think they'd get one thin dime from you – so why not negotiate a deal? You'll be in the best position to do this if you have the money available to pay off the balance in full (with that balance being a *reduced* balance that you have negotiated) when you initiate the

call, but worst case scenario is that you set-up a payment plan.

3) Always, always, always get the deal in writing.

4) Never, never, never give the collection agency your checking account or debit card info (because I believe in staying in control!).

5) Keep careful records and keep a log of your discussions (date, who you spoke with at the company including first and last name, or employee ID number, if they won't give out names, and the specific details that you agreed upon).

6) Ask that your payments be recorded with the credit reporting agencies.

7) Send all payments by certified mail with a return receipt.

Keep all of these records with your important documents. You wouldn't believe how many times I worked with mortgage clients who claimed they had paid collection accounts in full, but had no records to prove it.

Yes, I'm a "paper trail" kind of girl – and that documentation has served me well on many occasions.

This will also be extremely useful information when you start repairing your credit score.

The Maintenance Plan

I know, the term "maintenance plan" sounds like something straight out of a weight loss book. But in fact, we need to talk about how you will keep your finances on track from this point forward.

You've worked too darn hard to get to this point to take any financial steps backwards. We're not playing "Shoots and Ladders" here – this is your life.

These are some ideas to help you with that mission:

1) Track your *net worth* each month

Let's talk about your net worth. I believe it is powerful to calculate your net worth each month (and it is so much fun to watch it grow!).

Your Net Worth = Assets – Liabilities

That's a fancy way of saying that we will take everything you own that has a value – a house, car, boat, artwork, jewelry, etc., and add up what it is worth in the marketplace. We also look at what you have as investments – your retirement accounts, your savings, stock, etc., and figure out its value. These are all of your assets.

Next, we look at everything you owe – the balance on your mortgage, any loans against the car or boat, and the list of debts that are not yet paid off.

Think of it as the "If I died tomorrow, what would my heirs inherit" list.

When you have a boatload of debt, a home that is mortgaged up to (or beyond) its value, and little, if any, savings – chances are pretty good that your net worth is a big fat negative number.

Every month, as your savings grow and your debts decrease, *your net worth will also increase.* Do you want to go to your grave, leaving the cost of your funeral to somebody else, or would you feel good about passing along a nice little "nest egg" (why do they call it that) to the people you love?

Keeping that in mind will help you stay focused to grow your net worth.

2) Keep the systems that you learned in this book in place.

Systems such as opening the mail regularly and scheduling a regular time each week to deal with your bills. And, keeping a log of money that flows to you. And, paying off your debts from lowest minimum payment to highest minimum payment, and rolling the payment forward to the next bill.

I recommend that you review this book often to remind yourself what you've implemented, and to keep the systems that we developed in placed.

3) Always track your finances on your Financial Freedom Worksheet.

The minute you stop monitoring your financial status – when you stop paying attention – you will start to let those old habits start creeping back into your life.

Again, you've worked too hard to turn your financial life around. You have to watch your finances – now, and for the rest of your life.

4) Make good financial decisions, and don't make them hastily.

Each time you even consider taking on a debt, crunch the numbers. Look at your new financial scenario with an additional bill. Will you have to reduce the amount you are saving to stay at break even if you take on this debt? Will it slow you down paying off another bill? And most important, ask yourself, *"Do I really **need** this?"*

5) Work as a team.

If you have a spouse, significant other, or partner in your life, work with them as a team. Certainly you may have some terse moments, but stay focused on your future, and your goal to be financially free.

And what the heck, making decisions about your finances *together* – especially when you have the *"want versus need"* discussions may have a positive impact on your relationship.

Depending on the age of your children, you might consider involving the entire family. Wouldn't it be powerful to teach your children great money management principles at an early age?

6) Set-up automatic payments

I'm a big fan of setting up regular bills on auto payments. Time them so they come out of your checking account right after your deposits come in.

I think it's important to be the one "in control" on auto pay – so I never give a creditor my account info.

Each week, I set-up the payments to go automatically out from my checking account. I'm in control, and you should be, too.

One thing I did to manage things a bit easier was to split my rent (or mortgage) payment in half, paying half out of each paycheck. This helped me manage finances easier, since my rent payment was my largest payment due each month.

One word of caution: if you choose to do the same, make sure when you implement the half payments that you are a half-month "ahead" of the due date, so you don't end up with a late fee (or nasty note from your landlord).

When I asked my landlord about making half rental payments, I started by making a "half rent" payment on March 15th for the rent

that was due on April 1st. That way, when I made the second "half rent" payment on April 1st, my rent was paid in full.

7) Continue to give yourself imaginary gold stamps

When you have created a huge financial mess, digging yourself out isn't easy. That's why it is so important to pat yourself on the back with every step that you make.

Once in a while, you might slip up. Just like a dieter "cheats" by eating a hot fudge sundae, people in debt "cheat" once in a while by buying a CD or throwing a couple extras into the cart at the grocery store.

As long as these "slip ups" don't become "regular occurrences," there is no need to beat yourself up.

Cash in some of those "imaginary gold stamps" and move on.

8) Reward yourself! I suggest that you reward yourself as you make progress and follow plan – not by spending money or eating, but rather by doing something special – whatever would feel like a "treat" or "reward" for you and your family. Just don't choose something that will drain your checking account (or require you to take money from savings – remember that's for *emergencies* only).

9) Two things that you should continue to focus on now (while you're in the "digging out" phase) and will become extremely important as you build wealth and financial

freedom are: a) continue your "money attraction" log, and b) save at least 10-percent of every penny you attract.

10) As you start to build a surplus - meet with qualified financial advisors to start building your wealth. They will get you on a solid plan that will help you meet your financial goals.

Final Thoughts from Susie ...

My goal in writing this book was to provide a step-by-step plan that teaches people how to dig themselves out of a financial mess. If I was able to dig out from the financial disaster that I created for myself, then anyone can do the same.

This isn't a book about getting rich, although turning your "financial Titanic" around is the first step of that process.

Some additional advice I'd like to share with you, based on lessons that I learned as I transformed my financial life:

1) Life isn't fair – stop playing the victim. That was a tough one for me to figure out. I wasted a lot of energy over the years being upset if someone got something I didn't. Get over it – now – and move on!

2) Stop buying lottery tickets, going to casinos, or hoping for a big inheritance. It is much more powerful to build wealth yourself. In fact, I keep this note posted in several locations, so I see it several times each day:

"I am a self-made multi-millionaire."

3) You are more powerful than you ever imagined. You will discover that by taking the kind of focused action that is detailed in this book. If you don't believe me, you will when you look back at what you accomplished as you took control of your finances.

4) Pity Parties are a drag, and few people show up! You can choose to get up each day and smear yourself with the doom and gloom of your poor pathetic life, or you can do something about it by taking action. As I said early on in this book – if you need professional help, get it. Otherwise, get the lead out of your butt and change your circumstances.

5) You can't fix your finances all at once, but at the same time – you can fix them faster than you think. I desperately tried to "fix it all" too quickly, and it usually made matters worse. Once I understood that the way to solve my financial problems once and for all was by implementing a plan, it helped me stay on track.

6) Visualize every single day what your life will be like when you are debt-free. Think about how it will feel. See how your life will be different. This will also help you achieve the goal faster.

7) Decide you want to be rich. The first step to any achievement is making a clear decision about what you really really want. Make that decision now.

8) Be a continual student. Feed your mind with ideas, techniques, and information.

About the Author

Susie Nelson built and maintained one of the top organizations in her home party sales company and became its second Independent National Sales Manager (a level that was only reached by six consultants in the history of the U.S. company).

From the day she made the decision and commitment to build her business and organization to the top level in her company, and to create a six-figure+ residual annual income, Susie focused her efforts, developed and implemented a strategic plan, and created systems to build her business quickly.

All of those efforts paid off. Here's just some of Susie Nelson's accomplishments:

- Under Susie's direction, her organization achieved her company's "Circle of Excellence" award every single year. To do that, a unit had to achieve at least $650,000 in sales. Eight of those years, her unit exceeded $1 Million in sales, and one year – they even exceeded $2 Million in sales.

- Susie promoted the most sales managers of anyone in the U.S. company – 16 to be exact. (To become a sales manager, you had to build and maintain a unit of at least 20 party plan consultants, and exceed $7000 wholesale production per month.) She also inspired 2 women to become sales managers indirectly (meaning, one of her off-spring managers promoted those managers within 12 months of becoming a sales manager herself).

- She became her home party sales company's 2nd National Sales Manager (only six managers achieved this level). This level was achieved when you promoted at least 10 sales managers from your unit.

- Susie was awarded the company's President's Award (based on production, growth, attitude, and votes from her peers) twice. This award was only given to four consultants per year – so to receive this recognition twice was an incredible honor.

- In 1996, Susie was also recognized for "Most Sales Manager Promotions" for promoting out 6 sales managers in a single year – a record that was never broken. She is extremely proud of this accomplishment – because she believes that home party and network marketing businesses are built by coaching, training and mentoring others. Many of her off-spring managers went on to build Million Dollar and $650,000 units themselves.

- Susie built and maintained a 6-figure income ($105,000 to $135,000) for 11 years straight! Not many consultants in the party plan industry achieve that level of financial success. She credits implementing a smart, well-planned business strategy, along with creating systems in her business for helping her develop a strong organization.

She has also worked on the corporate side of the business – for 3 different start-up companies, doing everything from developing comprehensive training programs, field development, and marketing.

Susie is the author of 4 books:

"I Did It, and You Can, Too: How to Build a Six Figure Direct Sales Business in Just 15 Hours Per Week." (Available on Kindle, or PDF)

"The Pros and Cons of Building More than One Direct Sales Business: What You Must Consider Before You Sign with a Second (or Third!) Company." (Available on Kindle, or PDF)

"8 Weeks to Your Promotion In Your Home Party Business: How to Rapidly Qualify for a Promotion, and Get Paid at Title Every Single Month."

"From Drowning in Debt to Financial Freedom: How to Bail Yourself Out of a Financial Mess by Building a Home Party or Network Marketing Business."

Now Susie has a new goal: To help at least 1000 home party consultants build a six-figure business, using her proven systems and strategies.

Recommended Resources

Susie Nelson's training program for home party and network marketing consultants.
Go to: SusieNelson-training.com,
SixFigureHomePartyBusiness.com

Books:

- The Total Money Makeover: Classic Edition: A Proven Plan for Financial Fitness by Dave Ramsey

- The Richest Man in Babylon – by George S. Clason

- The New Psycho-Cybernetics – by Maxwell Maltz, MD, FICS – Edited and Updated by Dan Kennedy

- Creating Affluence –by Deepak Chopra

- The Science of Getting Rich – Wallace D. Wattles

- The Millionaire Next Door – by Thomas J. Stanley

- Rich Dad, Poor Dad – by Robert Kyosaki

- Make Money – Not Excuses – by Jean Chatzky

- The 9 Steps to Financial Freedom – by Suze Orman

- You're Broke Because You Want to Be – by Larry Winget

45522707R00116

Made in the USA
Charleston, SC
25 August 2015